FOLDING
TECHNIQUES
FOR
Paul Jackson
DESIGNERS
FROM SHEET
TO FORM

Laurence King Publishing

CONTENTS

Preface

As a teenager, my favourite hobby was origami. Later, as a student of fine art, a steady flow of my original designs was published and I became a very minor player among the small international community of origami creators. Friends who were taking courses in graphic design or industrial design occasionally asked me for origami ideas to help with their projects, and I even did a little teaching.

In 1981, I finished my postgraduate studies in London. Out in the real world and needing a job, I had an idea: maybe courses in art and design in the London area would welcome a short course on origami? I had nothing to lose except the cost of the postage, so I sent a proposal to more than a hundred courses, unsure of the response I would receive.

A few days later the phone started to ring. And ring. Within weeks I was teaching students of fashion design, textile design, graphic design and jewellery design, pleased to be working.

But there was one problem: I had no idea what to teach! Certainly I was skilled at origami, and I had excellent experience in higher education, but my subject had been fine art and I didn't understand what I should teach to students of design. I was entirely ignorant of what design students learnt. Also, my hobbyist's knowledge of origami was confined to models – that is, representations of flora, fauna, objects and geometric forms. The one thing I did know was that students of art and design didn't need to learn how to make an origami giraffe.

I have always admitted that my first attempts at teaching students of design were terrible. In those early days I did little more than use selections from a list of favourite models. Slowly, though, I began to understand something that now seems very obvious to me, but which at the time required a quantum leap of my imagination – namely, that I shouldn't be teaching the students how to make origami models, but instead, should teach them how to fold. It had never previously occurred to me that folding paper was anything other than model making. To understand that origami could be as much about folding as about models seemed a radical departure. In time, I came to realize that it wasn't radical at all, but a consequence of being unwittingly blinkered – brainwashed, even – by 15 years of origami practice.

The crucial educational difference was that a model was simply a model – perhaps fun to learn, but it didn't teach the students much that they could apply creatively to their design work. By contrast, if folding techniques were taught, they could be used with any number of different materials and adapted to any number of design applications. And when I looked around, I could find examples of folding throughout both the natural and the designed worlds.

That revelation was the genesis of this book.

In the few years following that epiphany, I evolved a series of self-contained mini workshops that introduced a diversity of folding techniques – pleating, crumpling, one crease and so on. I would shuffle the choice and content of the workshops to best suit each course. The workshops were usually followed by quick 'hit and run' creative projects.

As word spread, I began to be employed as a consultant by a number of multinational companies, to give workshops on the theory and practice of folding. I also gave workshops to a variety of design practices and to architects, structural engineers and professional bodies. These experiences fed back into my teaching, which in turn fed back into my professional experiences.

By the late 1980s, the final form of my teaching had more or less evolved. I have taught what I came to call 'Sheet to Form' workshops and projects to students of fashion, textiles (surface, print, knit and weave), ceramics, embroidery, product design, industrial design, engineering, architecture, jewellery, graphic design, interior design, environmental design, model-making, packaging, theatre design, fine art, printmaking, foundation courses – and probably other courses now forgotten – at all educational levels, from my local community college in north London, to the Royal College of Art and colleges in Germany, the US, Israel, Belgium and Canada. To date, I've taught on more than 150 courses in design in 54 colleges, some regularly for a decade or more, others for just a day.

Wherever I've taught, I've always been asked the same question: "Is this in a book?" My answer was always "No!" and, frankly, the lack of follow-up material, or any substantial documentation, was an embarrassment to me. Although there are hundreds of origami books, they are all about model-making, of limited use to a design student or professional. My best advice was always to keep carefully the samples made in the workshop and refer to them when working on a project.

So, finally … finally! … I have the opportunity to present in print the most useful of my Sheet to Form workshops. Deciding what to include or exclude, or to emphasize or skim over, has been difficult and time-consuming, and I hope I have made the right choices. I have written more than 30 books about origami and paper crafts, but this is the one I have most wanted to write.

Perhaps, though, it was proper that the book was not written until now. In recent years there has been an upsurge of interest in origami, not only by designers of all disciplines, but also by mathematicians, scientists, educators and others. 'Origami' and 'folding' are very much words of our time, and though the focus will doubtless diminish, the interest and respect will remain. This book, then, is being published at the right time.

I hope that while using this book you will come to share my enthusiasm and love for a subject that I have come to regard simply as a Wholly Good Thing. I feel very privileged that it has not only made me a living, but given me an absorbing and fulfilling life and introduced me to many wonderful people, worldwide.

Paul Jackson

00. Symbols

The few symbols shown here recur throughout the book.
Some of them occur on almost every drawing. Please take
a little time to familiarize yourself with them, so that you
can fold fluently and accurately.

1. Valley fold

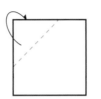

2. Mountain fold

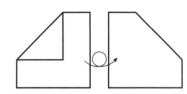

3. Turn over

4. Unfolded
valley fold

5. Unfolded
mountain fold

6. Bring these
points together

7. Glue here

8. Mark this fold

9. Universal fold

Introduction

All designers fold.

That is, all designers crease, pleat, bend, hem, gather, knot, hinge, corrugate, drape, twist, furl, crumple, collapse, wrinkle, facet, curve or wrap two-dimensional sheets of material, and by these processes of folding, create three-dimensional objects. These objects will perhaps not be origami-like in appearance, or the folding may only be a detail, but most will nevertheless have been folded – wholly or in part – in some way. Since almost all objects are made from sheet materials (such as fabric, plastic, sheet metal or cardboard), or are fabricated from components used to make sheet forms (such as bricks – a brick wall is a sheet form), folding can be considered one of the most common of all design techniques.

And yet, despite being so ubiquitous, folding as a design topic is rarely studied. Perhaps this is because the folded content in a designed object is often unrecognized, or merely incidental, or because folding is synonymous with origami, with brightly coloured squares and children's hobbycrafts (an image of origami now several decades out of date). Folding is rarely an inspiration for designers.

At least, that is how it used to be. In recent years, more and more designers of all disciplines have turned to folding to create a wide range of handmade and manufactured objects, both functional and decorative. A little time spent looking through design and style magazines will reveal a significant number of folded products, from apparel to lighting and from architecture to jewellery. Origami is one of the most vibrant buzzwords in contemporary design.

Folding Techniques for Designers is the first book to present this essential topic specifically to designers. For almost 30 years, I have specialized in teaching folding techniques to design students and to design professionals of all disciplines, perhaps the only such specialist teacher since the days of the Bauhaus, when Josef Albers taught paper folding as a basic topic of design.

Chapter by chapter this book presents those techniques which, from my experience, have proven to be the most inspirational and the most versatile. It comprehensively describes the basics, including such diverse techniques as pleating, crumpling and box making, presenting concepts variously as step-by-step drawing sequences, crease pattern diagrams and photographs. The techniques are presented in paper, but the reader is encouraged to adapt them freely, using other sheet materials. This book is not primarily a book about paper or paper folding, but a book about folding.

The aim of the book is to establish folding as a primary design tool and, by doing so, to reintroduce it as an essential topic in design education and design practice.

How to Use the Book

The book presents generic folding concepts from which ideas for designed products can be derived. It is not a book of models to copy, or of formulaic design solutions. This book is useful – or should be – because it presents practical concepts of folding that can be adapted infinitely by any designer from any design discipline, using any sheet material.

It presents the basic ways in which a sheet of 100gsm paper can be manipulated into three-dimensional forms or relief surfaces. It does not show how those concepts can be adapted to thousands of other sheet materials which are thicker, thinner, softer, harder, larger or smaller, which are stitched, glued or self-supporting, which are one-piece or multi-piece, which are hand-made or machine-made, which are rigid or flexible, pervious or impervious, tough and hard-wearing or delicate and decorative ...and so on and so on, without end. These are decisions that you must make as a designer.

As you work through the book and look at the diagrams and photographs, you will hopefully remark time and again "That's obvious". But you would be wrong! Generic concepts are necessarily 'obvious', but usually only so after they have been seen. Each chapter is devoted to a technical theme and the many illustrated variations – some of them apparently almost identical – have been carefully selected to show the different ways in which a technique can be employed. Only when you make and play with them will these differences become apparent.

The key word in that last sentence is 'play'. In fact, it is the key word to using the book successfully. Do not just make an example, look at it briefly, then turn the page to make something different. Instead, play with it. Bend it this way and that; press together the folds along one edge, then along another edge, then press two edges together at the same time; invert it (that is, 'pop' it inside out); squeeze the middle; try to make the opposite corners touch and turn it around and around in your two hands to look at it from all angles. Many of the examples in the book, although apparently rigid when seen in a photograph, have the flexibility of an Olympic gymnast. It is your choice whether what you design is flexible or rigid.

Do not be seduced into making only the more complex examples. Also make the simpler, less showy ones because they will offer you more creative possibilities in a greater choice of materials. When folding, as in all matters of design, less is often more (more or less). The Basic Concepts chapter is extremely important. The concepts it introduces can be freely adapted to anything described in any subsequent chapter. Pick an example at random from any chapter and imagine how it would change if it were adapted to any or all of the concepts in the Basic Concepts chapter. But do not just imagine what they would look like – make as many as you can. If you cannot understand how to make something you thought of, try anyway. You may not make it exactly, but you may well make something different and better, which you did not (or could not) conceive of when you began.

Of course, not everything extrapolated from the examples in the book will be immediately successful. Much of what you create initially will probably be technically or aesthetically weak. However, some pieces will be more satisfactory, while others will become successful after a process of much refinement. In this sense, folding paper is no different to any other design process. It is not a 'quick fix' substitute for perseverance and hard work.

In truth, there is absolutely no substitute for folding, folding, folding. Thinking too much, analyzing too much and trying to understand in your head what something will look like will inevitably lead you to poor design work. Paper is readily available, quick and easy to work with, and very inexpensive. Use it – and use this book – as extensively as time permits before perhaps adapting your ideas for use with other materials.

How to Make the Examples

There are four ways to make the examples you see in the book. Which method you use for which example depends on personal taste and on the characteristics of the example being made.

Like developing ideas in a sketchbook, the key to developing good designs in folded paper is to work fluently and quickly. Your folding does not always need to be technically perfect (yes, really!). A great deal of time can be saved by working somewhat roughly, then remaking something with care when you feel you have an idea worth developing. Do not allow yourself to become bogged down in unnecessarily precise folding, when all you need is a quickly made folded sketch. Working too slowly is typical of a beginner. With experience, your speed and spontaneity with paper will increase.

1. Folding by hand

Folding by hand is as low-tech as any making activity can be. You are making something directly with your body (your hands) without the intervention of a third-party tool such as a pencil, mouse or needle. It is an almost unique making experience and perhaps unfamiliarly primal. This very basic, hands-on activity – especially in today's high-tech design studio environments – can be a very powerful and rewarding experience for both the rawest student and the most seasoned professional, and should not be underestimated or regarded as unsophisticated or inadequate. You can think of folding by hand as an alternative to designing by computer (which means that aside from the design benefits, folding by hand is of itself an excellent educational experience).

Many of the examples in the book are made from paper divided into 8, 16 or 32. These divisions are quick and easy to make by hand (see pages 16–18 of the Basic Concepts chapter), and learning how to make them will save you a great deal of time measuring with a ruler.

Think of folding by hand as the norm, and resort to using the other methods described below only when necessary.

2. Using geometry equipment to draw the folds

Simple geometry equipment such as a scalpel or craft knife, ruler, pair of compasses, 360° protractor and a hard, sharp pencil is sometimes necessary to help construct unusual shapes of paper, precise angles, incremental divisions etc. However, be careful that using them does not become habitual, so that you find yourself using them when folding something by hand would be quicker and easier.

To make a fold using a scalpel or craft knife, turn the blade over and make the crease line by running the back of the blade against the side of a ruler. Never try to cut through some of the thickness of the paper to create a fold; just compress it with the back of the blade.

3. Using a computer to draw the folds

These days, most of us would prefer to draw folding patterns on a computer rather than draw them on paper with geometry equipment. We seem to be losing the hands-on habit. However, drawing on a computer does have its advantages: scaling is easy, as is symmetrical repetition, or skewing and stretching, and drawings can be kept and copied endlessly.

The biggest drawback is having to print out your drawing. If the drawing is bigger than the size of your printer, you may have to collage sections together, which can be messy and imprecise. The alternative is to use a plotter. If you do not have ready access to one, many walk-in print and copy shops have a plotter and can make inexpensive black-and-white copies a metre or so wide.

4. A combination of the above methods

Being pragmatic and switching between the three methods described above is probably the way that most people will make most of the examples, most of the time. Each has its advantages and disadvantages, and experience will tell you which method to use, and when.

How to Work from the Drawings, Photographs and the Text

The Drawings

Unless stated in the text, the exact lengths and angles used in a drawing are unimportant. As long as what you make looks something like the drawing, it will be accurate enough. Where an element of the construction is critical, this will be stated and you should follow the instructions exactly. If a shape is clearly a circle (or whatever), this may not be stated, so do the obvious and make what your eyes can see. Think of the drawings as suggestions rather than as models to copy.

However, rather than 'eyeball' a drawing and draw it freehand without references, it may be helpful to first use a ruler and measure the major lines of a drawing. This will give you a rough sense of its proportion, and then it can be scaled up to the appropriate size.

One tip when making something for the first time is not to make it very small. Samples that are small can look trivial and be creatively inhibiting, and you can feel that your time has been wasted. Similarly, if you make things too big they can look clumsy and weak. As a rough guide, try to make samples that can fit on to an A4 sheet. Later, when you know the scale you want and the sheet material you want to work with, you can make them at the correct scale, larger or smaller.

The Photographs

Although the photographs were taken to make the examples look interesting and attractive (of course), their primary function is to give descriptive information about how the different planes, edges and folds lie in relation to each other, so that you have a better sense of how something should look when made. In that sense, the photographs should be regarded as diagrams, not simply as pleasing pictures that beautify the book.

Paper is a living, breathing material. It distorts under the heat of studio lights, reacts to humidity and can bend out of symmetry, depending on the direction of the grain (the parallel fibres that lie within the paper). For these reasons, some of the folded examples may look a little misshapen. The alternative to seeing an occasional wobble was to make everything from thick card that would not distort. However, this was considered a rather soulless material for the book. The idiosyncrasies of paper are hopefully more appealing, giving the folded forms a little personality.

The Text
In three words – please read it!

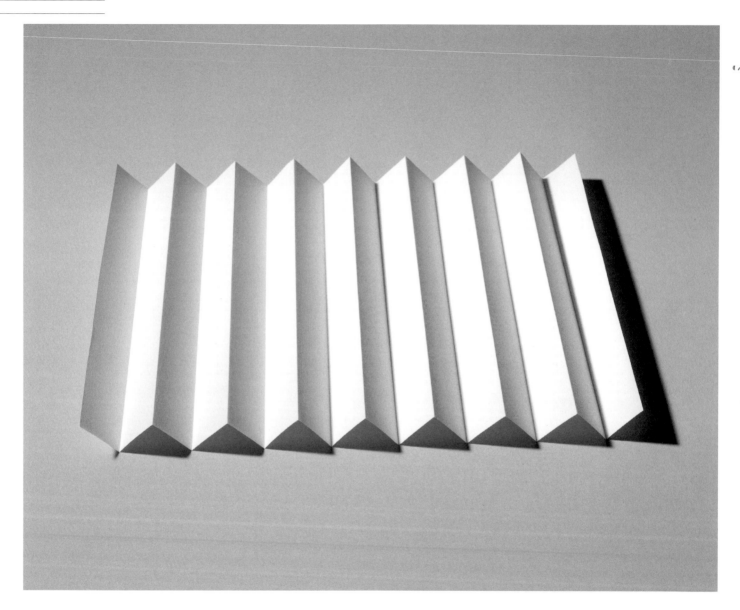

1.1.1 Linear Divisions into sixteenths

1.   Basic Concepts

Basics are basics. What was basic yesterday will be basic tomorrow. Basics are the constants, the unchanging foundations upon which creative work can be built.

This chapter explains the basics of folding paper. The general concepts it introduces are the most important and the most useful in the book. Time spent learning them will be well rewarded when you progress to later chapters and when you create your own folded designs. If you are new to folding, or have only limited experience, you are encouraged to spend quality time with this chapter. However, do not just look at its contents — fold them!

Basic concepts are not only useful, but are also very adaptable. This is because they are necessarily generic and can thus be modified in an infinite number of ways. By contrast, ideas for folding which are more specific, are less adaptable. So, somewhat paradoxically, this is perhaps the book's least showy chapter, but it also offers the most creativity. 'Basic' should not be mistaken for 'uncreative'.

1.1.   Dividing the Paper

Dividing paper into exactly equal lengths or angles enables many other techniques to be performed. The position of the folds can be marked with a ruler and pencil, but it is much quicker and much more accurate to make them by hand, dividing the paper into halves, then quarters, then eighths...and so on, using a simple and precise sequence of folds. It is the hand-made method that is explained here.

There is nothing inherently special about the sixteenths, thirty-seconds or sixty-fourths shown in this section, other than that they divide the paper many times and are easy divisions to explain. In your own work, it may be that you need to divide the paper into tenths, twenty-sixths, fifty-fourths, or whatever, in which case it is better to divide it into 16, 32 or 64 and then trim off the excess. Do not be a slave to the divisions shown here.

1.1.1. Linear Divisions: Sixteenths

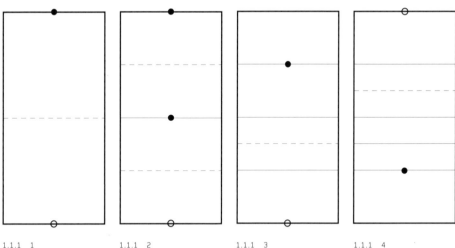

1.1.1 _ 1
Fold the o edge to the ● edge, folding the paper in half. Open the paper.

1.1.1 _ 2
Fold the edges to the centre line. Open the paper.

1.1.1 _ 3
Fold the o edge to the ● crease. Open the paper.

1.1.1 _ 4
Repeat Step 3 with the other edge.

1.   BASIC
CONCEPTS

1.1.   **Dividing
the Paper**

1.1.1.   Linear Divisions:
Sixteenths

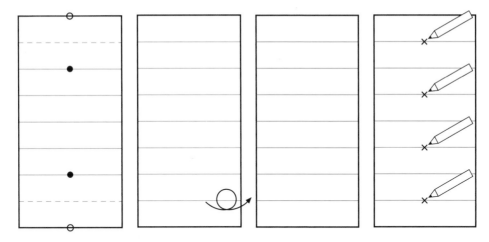

1.1.1 _ 5
Fold the o edges to the ● creases. Open the paper.

1.1.1 _ 6
There are now seven valley folds that divide the paper into equal eighths. Turn the paper over.

1.1.1 _ 7
There are now seven mountain folds.

1.1.1 _ 8
With a pencil, discreetly mark each alternate mountain crease.

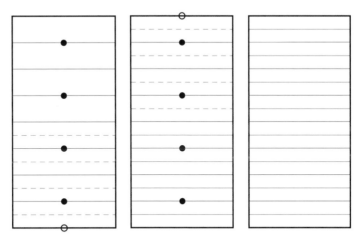

1.1.1 _ 9
Fold the o edge in turn to all the ● creases marked in Step 8, making four new folds. Open the paper after each new fold.

1.1.1 _ 10
Repeat Step 9 with the other edge of the paper.

1.1.1 _ 11
The paper is now divided into equal sixteenths, using creases which alternate mountain-valley-mountain-valley... across the paper (see photo on page 14).

1.   BASIC
     CONCEPTS

1.1.   **Dividing
       the Paper**

1.1.1. Linear Thirty-
        seconds

1.1.1   Linear Thirty-seconds

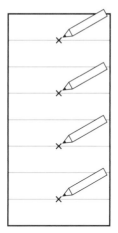
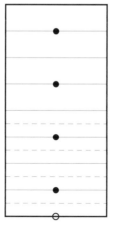
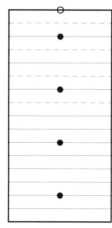
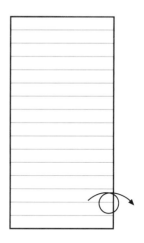

1.1.1 _ 1
Begin with Step 6 of the
Linear Sixteenths method
(see page 17). Using a
pencil, discreetly mark each
alternate valley crease.

1.1.1 _ 2
Fold the o edge in turn to
all the ● creases marked
in Step 1, making four new
folds. Open the paper after
each new fold.

1.1.1 _ 3
Repeat Step 2 with the
other edge of the paper.

1.1.1 _ 4
There are now 15 valley
folds. Turn the paper over.

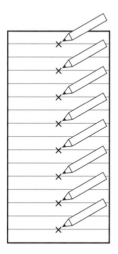
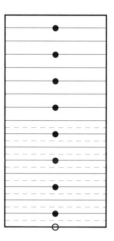
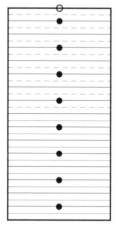

1.1.1 _ 5
With a pencil, discreetly
mark each alternate
mountain crease.

1.1.1 _ 6
Fold the o edge in turn to
all the ● creases marked
in Step 5, making eight
new folds. Open the paper
after each new fold.

1.1.1 _ 7
Repeat Step 6 with the
other edge of the paper.

1.1.1 _ 8
The paper is now divided
into equal thirty-seconds,
using creases which
alternate mountain-
valley-mountain-valley
(see photo opposite).

BASIC
CONCEPTS
.1.   **Dividing
the Paper**
.1.1. Linear Thirty-
seconds

1.1.1. Linear Divisions into thirty-seconds

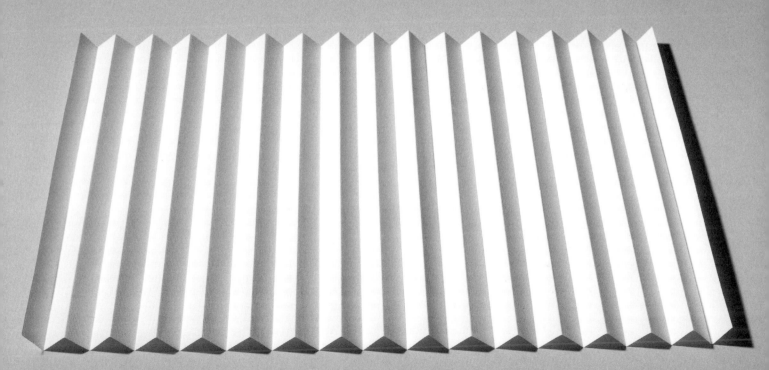

1.1.1. Linear Sixty-fourths

To divide the paper into 64, fold up to Step 4 of the Linear Thirty-seconds method (see page 18). Then, instead of turning the paper over, continue on the same side, completing all the thirty-seconds as valley folds. Now turn the paper over. Mark the alternate mountain folds and make valleys between the mountains by folding the edges to the marked creases. This will complete the division into sixty-fourths.

If a piece of paper is first divided into equal thirds rather than in half, it can then be divided into accurate sixths, twelfths, twenty-fourths and so on, which may be more useful than 16, 32 or 64.

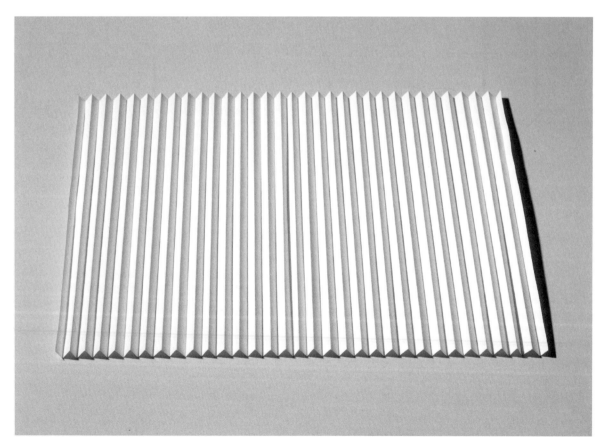

1.1.1 Linear Divisions into sixty-fourths

.. BASIC
CONCEPTS

..1. **Dividing
the Paper**

..1.2. Rotational
Divisions:
Sixteenths

1.1.2.   Rotational Divisions: Sixteenths

1.1.2 _ 1
Divide the paper into two
90° angles by folding the
o edge to the ● edge.
Open the paper.

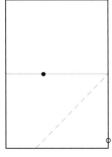

1.1.2 _ 2
Fold the o edge to the ●
crease. Open the paper.

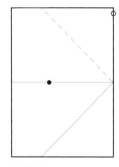

1.1.2 _ 3
Repeat Step 2 with the top
half of the paper. Open
the paper.

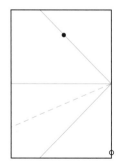

1.1.2 _ 4
Fold the o edge to the ●
crease. Open the paper.

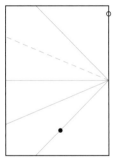

1.1.2 _ 5
Repeat Step 4 with the
top half of the paper.
Open the paper.

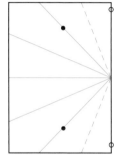

1.1.2 _ 6
Fold the o edges to the ●
creases. There are now
seven valley folds and
eight equal angles.

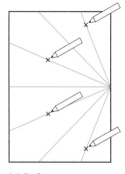

1.1.2 _ 7
On the reverse side of
the paper, discreetly mark
each alternate mountain
crease with a pencil.

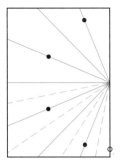

1.1.2 _ 8
Fold the o edge in turn to
all the ● creases marked
in Step 7, making four new
folds. Open the paper after
each new fold.

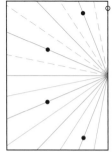

1.1.2 _ 9
Repeat Step 8 with the
top half of the paper.

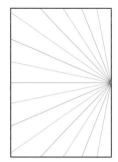

1.1.2 _ 10
The paper has now been
divided into 16 equal
angles, using creases
which alternate mountain-
valley-mountain-valley (see
photo overleaf on page 22).

1. BASIC
CONCEPTS

1.1. **Dividing
the Paper**

1.1.2. Rotational
Sixteenths
Variations

1.1.2. Rotational Sixteenths Variations

With Linear Sixteenths (see pages 16–17), the spacing between the parallel folds depends wholly on the length of the paper being divided. However, with Rotational Sixteenths, the spacing between the angled folds depends wholly on the number of degrees of paper around the point where all the folds meet.

Here are some further examples. The methods of construction are identical to the Rotational Sixteenths method (see page 21).

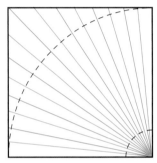

1.1.2 _11
An angle of 90° is divided
into sixteenths.

1.	BASICS
	CONCEPTS
1.1.	**Dividing**
	the Paper
1.1.2.	Rotational
	Sixteenths
	Variations

1.1.2 _ 12

1.1.2 _ 12
An angle of 360° is divided into sixteenths. The angle can be increased to 720° if two identical sheets are prepared and folded as shown, then overlapped and glued together, rather like the shavings from a sharpened pencil. When the folds from this 720° surface are bunched up, they will sit flat in a 360° arc. More than two sheets may be glued together for even greater angles.

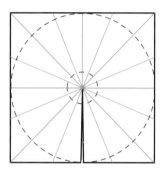

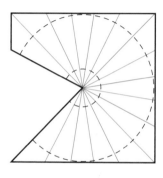

1.1.2 _ 13
An arbitrary angle is divided into sixteenths (see photo opposite).

BASIC
CONCEPTS
.1.   **Dividing
the Paper**
.1.2   Rotational
Sixteenths
Variations

1.1.2 _ 13. Rotational divisions into sixteenths

1.   BASIC
      CONCEPTS

1.1. **Dividing
      the Paper**

1.1.2. Rotational
        Thirty-seconds

1.1.2.   Rotational Thirty-seconds

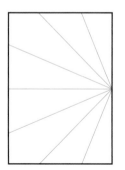 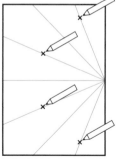 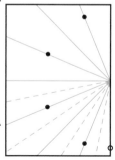 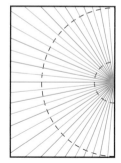

1.1.2 _ 14
Begin with Step 6 of the
Rotational Sixteenths
method (see page 21).

1.1.2 _ 15
With a pencil, discreetly
mark each alternate
valley crease.

1.1.2 _ 16
Fold the o edge in turn to
all the ● creases, making
four new folds. Repeat for
the top half, then turn the
paper over.

1.1.2 _ 17
Continue, following exactly
the method described for
Linear Thirty-seconds
(see page 18).

1.1.2 _ 17

BASIC
CONCEPTS
1.   **Dividing
    the Paper**

1.3. Diagonal
       Divisions

1.1.3.   Diagonal Divisions

So far, this chapter has shown how to divide paper by always bringing an edge to an existing crease so that the divisions are parallel to the edge of the paper. However, it is equally possible to divide paper by always bringing a corner to an existing crease so that the divisions are parallel to the diagonal. The two methods of construction are exactly the same, but the results look very different.

The method shown here divides the paper into diagonal sixteenths, but the methods described previously to divide paper into 32 or 64 could also be used.

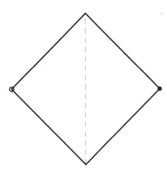

1.1.3 _ 1
Begin with a square of
paper. Fold the o corner
to the ● corner. Open
the paper.

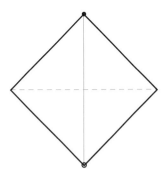

1.1.3 _ 2
Similarly, fold the o corner
to the ● corner, then open
the paper.

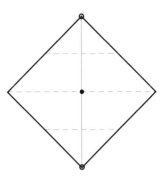

1.1.3 _ 3
Fold the o corners to the ●
intersection. Open the paper.
This will divide the vertical
diagonal into quarters. Turn
the paper over.

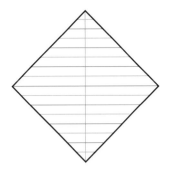

1.1.3 _ 4
Continue, following exactly
the method used for Linear
Sixteenths (see page 17).
The paper is now divided
into equal sixteenths, using
creases which alternate
mountain-valley-mountain-
valley along the length
of the vertical diagonal
(see photo overleaf).

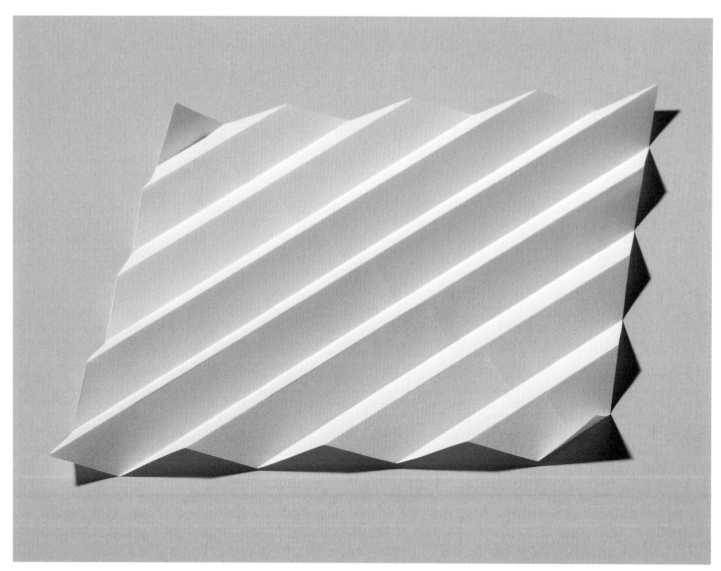

1.1.3 _ 4

1.1.4. Grid Divisions

The linear divisions described on pages 16–20 can follow more than one direction on the same sheet to create a grid of creases. There are too many possibilities to illustrate here, but most commonly, the two directions are perpendicular to each other and equally spaced, so that with square paper the grid becomes square.

It is also possible to create different divisions in the two directions (for example, eighths and sixteenths), so that the grid becomes rectangular, not square. Likewise, the paper can be rectangular, not square, to stretch or compress a grid.

Further, it is possible to superimpose two grids – most commonly, a grid parallel to the edges and a grid parallel to the diagonals – to create a dense multidirectional grid of great versatility.

Finally, by exchanging square or rectangular paper for paper of another shape – most commonly a hexagon – non-square and non-rectangular grids can be made. This 60° hexagonal geometry comprised of three lines of linear divisions that divide the paper into equilateral triangles (triangles in which all the angles are 60°) is just as versatile as the ubiquitous 90° grid, but is much, much less commonly used. The student of folding who is looking to develop new forms is well advised to take forms seen in 90° geometry and try to fold an equivalent with 60° geometry. If you have never folded and played with a 60° grid, try it – it is like entering a parallel universe of folding!

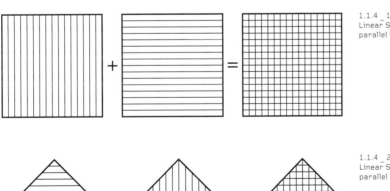

1.1.4 _ 1
Linear Sixteenths,
parallel to the edges.

1.1.4 _ 2
Linear Sixteenths,
parallel to the diagonals.

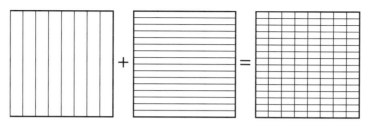

1.1.4 _ 3
Linear Eighths and Linear
Sixteenths, parallel to
the edges.

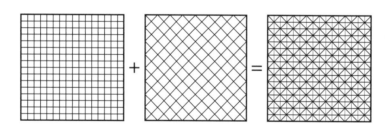

1.1.4 _ 4
Linear Eighths and Linear
Sixteenths, parallel to
the edges.

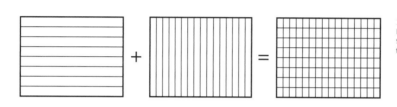

1.1.4 _ 5
Two grids (one parallel to
the edges and the other
parallel to the diagonals)
superimposed.

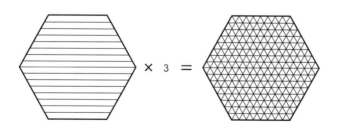

1.1.4 _ 6
Linear Sixteenths on
a hexagon, repeated
three times.

1.2.   Symmetrical Repeats

One way to describe a folded design is as a two-dimensional surface design of crease lines, given form. Any study of surface design will quickly introduce the topic of pattern, in which a motif is repeated in a regular arrangement. Folded forms are often made from repeat patterns, some are more easy to see than others.

The essence of pattern making, including crease patterns, is symmetry. There are four basic types of two-dimensional symmetry – translation, reflection, rotation and glide reflection – all of which can be used to great effect when developing new folded forms. An understanding of these four types will generate a remarkable number of usable crease patterns from even the simplest motif. Generating these patterns is a pencil and paper game, though of course there is no substitute for eventually folding the drawings to see what you have created.

1.2.1. Translation

Definition: a motif is repeated exactly in one direction.

This is the simplest form of symmetry. A motif is repeated in a straight line without overlap. When applied to a square of paper (or other polygon), the squares are simply repeated side by side and the crease pattern repeated.

Folded motif

1.2.1 _ 1
An example of
translation symmetry
(see photo overleaf).

Folded motif

1.2.1 _ 2
An example of
translation symmetry.

1.2.2. Reflection

**Definition: a motif is repeated exactly in one direction, but each time as
a mirror image of the preceding motif.**

Reflection symmetry makes possible crease patterns more complex than those
made with translation symmetry, because it becomes easier to connect motifs
together across the line of symmetry with a common crease.

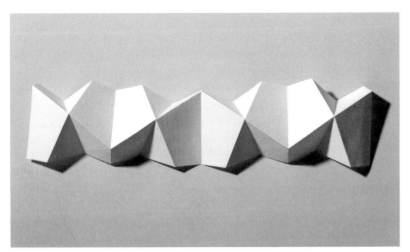

Folded motif

1.2.2 _ 1
An example of
reflection symmetry.

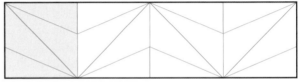

Folded motif

1.2.2 _ 2
An example of
reflection symmetry.

1.2.3.   Rotation

Definition: a motif is exactly repeated around one common point.

Unlike translation and reflection symmetries, which are linear repeats, rotation symmetry makes possible repetition across a plane, around a common point. Using a square, any of the four corners can be used as the common point of rotation, enabling many forms to be generated from the same motif.

1.2.3 _ 1 Motif 1 Variations

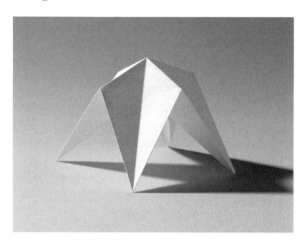

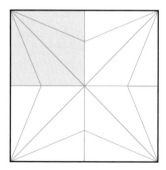

Folded motif

Repetition of the motif to create a star pattern of folds. The forms in the two photographs on the left are both folded from this single pattern. Each form is the other turned inside out.

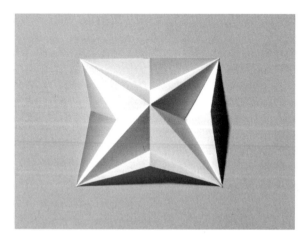

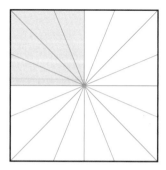

Repetition of the motif to create a radial pattern of folds. See photo opposite. Note that, like the example above and left, this form may also be turned inside out, though the difference is less dramatic.

BASIC
CONCEPTS
.2.   **Symmetrical
       Repeats**
.2.3. Rotation

1.2.3 _ 1

1.2.3 _ Motif 2 Variations

In both Motif 1 and Motif 2, many forms are possible, depending on how each form is collapsed. If a different corner of each motif is used as the common point of rotation, very different forms can be generated. Each rotational pattern of four motifs can itself be repeated around a common point to create surfaces and forms of great complexity and beauty, but from a simple motif.

1.2.3 _ 2/1

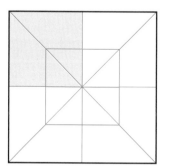

1.2.3 _ 2/2

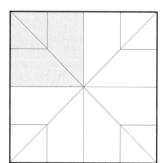

1.2.3 _ 2/1
In the two photos above, each form is the other turned inside out. They are both folded from this rotational configuration of the motif.

Folded motif

1.2.3 _ 2/2
Here the small, folded sqaure in the bottom right-hand corner of the motif is grouped with others around the centre to create a large, mountain-fold square which can be inverted into the paper. See photo opposite.

BASIC
CONCEPTS
.2.   **Symmetrical**
      Repeats
.2.3. Rotation

1.2.3 _ 2/2. Rotation symmetry

1.2.4.   Glide Reflection

Definition: a motif is translated and reflected, not necessarily in a straight line.

This is the most complex form of symmetry and the one which can take the most time to understand fully. The definition given above is the strictest and most correct definition, but it is often relaxed to include any combination of translation and reflection symmetries. Rules are made to be broken and glide reflection symmetry is a prime example of how designs can be evolved by learning and then disregarding what has been learnt. Essentially, anything goes, but respect, not disrespect, for the rules of symmetry will give you the tools to design patterns of glide reflection symmetry beyond those which are immediately obvious.

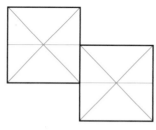

1.2.4 _ 1
In this simple example of glide reflection, the symmetry of the motif means that it is not apparently reflected. When the two-square motif is repeated across a plane, a complex and extraordinarily flexible surface is created, perhaps one of the most remarkable of all folded forms.
See photo on page 42.

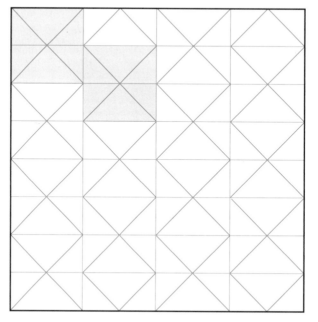

Here are some of the many forms which this motif can assume. Note that for extra flexibility this example has four times as many repeats as the diagrammed example opposite.

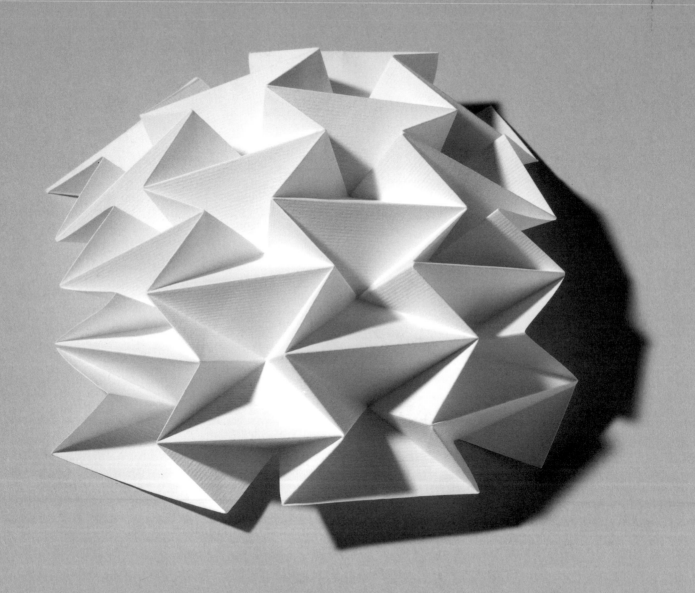

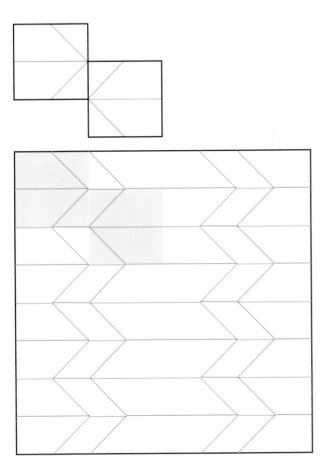

1.2.4 _ 2
Here, the glide reflection clearly includes a reflection.
However, the original motif has also been flipped front
to back, so that all the valley and mountain folds have
switched. When repeated across a plane, this complex
symmetry creates an interesting crease pattern in
which the symmetrical repeat is difficult to identify.

1.3.   Stretch and Skew

Stretching and skewing are two simple techniques which do not generate
new folded forms when applied, but which create variations of an original form,
perhaps better suited to design aspirations. The most natural paper shape to
use is a square, but a square might also be considered a cliché, even a tyranny.
To transform a square into another shape will transform a folded form into
something more bespoke and original.

Stretching and skewing can be combined very effectively with other basic
concepts in this chapter, to create forms that are two or three times removed
from an original crease pattern motif on a square of paper. These new folded
forms can be highly sophisticated and unusual or – frankly – they can be rather
contrived and tawdry. Only working with the paper in your hands will separate
the good results from the not so good.

1.3.1. Stretch

A square, when stretched in one specific direction, will create a rectangle.
Depending on the original crease pattern, the pattern will transform differently
if stretched vertically or horizontally, or it will transform in the same way in
whichever direction it is stretched.

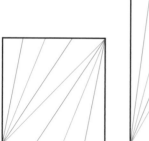 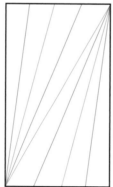 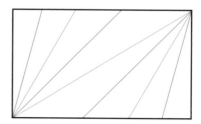

Examples: Set 1

The left-hand illustration above shows
a crease pattern made on a square.
That square is then stretched vertically
(centre illustration) and then horizontally
(right-hand illustration) to create
stretched variations. See the photos
on the opposite page.

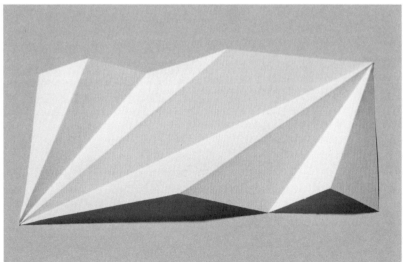

Examples: Set 2

In the same way as in Set 1 on page 44 a crease pattern made on a square is stretched vertically and horizontally. The photos below and opposite show how the folded form changes as a result of this process.

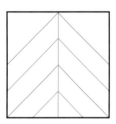
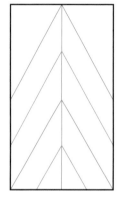
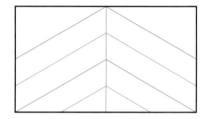

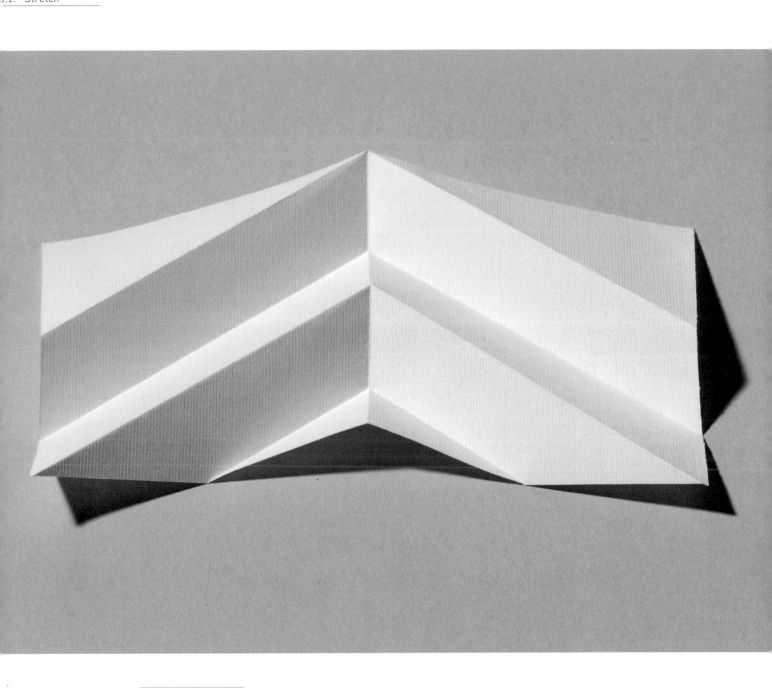

1.3.2.   Skew

A square skewed to one side will create opposite sides of equal length, but no angle of 90°. The transformations made to a form folded first in square paper are more dramatic than if the square is stretched first (see pages 44–47).

Examples: Set 1

This set takes Set 1 from the Stretch examples (see page 44) and skews the square motif first to the right and then to the left.

 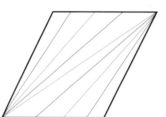 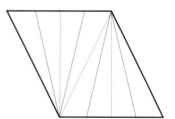

Examples: Set 2

This set takes Set 2 from
the Stretch examples (see
page 46) and skews the
square motif first to the
right and then to the left.
Two of the photos are on
this page. The third photo
is overleaf..

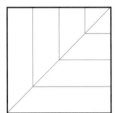 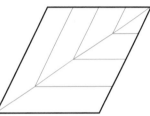 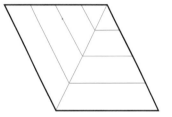

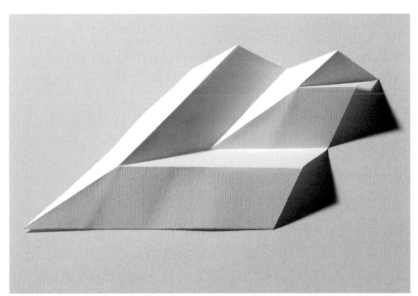

1.4.   Polygons

We live in a world of 90° corners. Look up from this book (which itself has 90° corners) and see how many you can find in your immediate surroundings – unless you are sitting under a shady tree surrounded by curvy nature, there are probably more than you would want to count. Occasionally, our choice of this shape is guided by manufacturing constraints or cost, but more often, it is made without thought, as though anything 90° is automatically right.

This automatic choice is also true when folding paper. Every type of paper comes with 90° corners. This is for very practical reasons – mostly concerned with the requirements of different printing processes – but when we fold paper as designers, these 90° corners need not be used at all, or even considered. We are free to use corners of any angle and, by extension, polygons with any number of sides, not just four.

To fold triangles, parallelograms, pentagons, hexagons, circles and papers of any irregular shape can be a liberating experience, but is also somewhat disorientating in our 90° world. However, if you are looking for ways to develop folded forms that don't use squares and rectangles, you are strongly encouraged to adapt them to non-90° polygons. Sometimes the results will not be worthwhile, but occasionally they will be superb – as always, diligent experimentation is the key to developing quality work.

1.4 _ 1
Here are a few examples
of polygons to consider
when developing new folded
forms. Most do not have
90° corners.

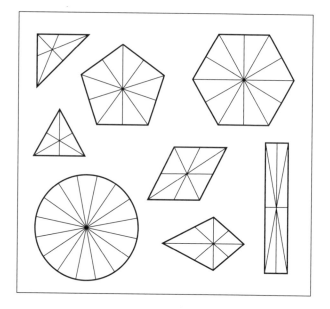

2.   Basic Pleats

Pleats are the most common, versatile and easy-to-use of all folding techniques. This chapter describes how to make the four basic types – Accordion, Knife, Box and Incremental pleats – and shows how even this basic knowledge can be used to create a great diversity of sophisticated surfaces and forms. Although clearly related, these four types of pleat create very different results, so it is worthwhile learning them all.

Techniques of folding are often interconnected. Some of the techniques in later chapters develop the basic pleat patterns introduced here, so time spent on this chapter will enable you to use much of the rest of the book.

The step-by-step diagrammatic instructions here assume a good knowledge of how to divide paper, explained in the 'Dividing the Paper' section (pages 16–30). If you have not read this section and folded the examples it contains, you are strongly recommended to do so before beginning this chapter. You can also use the information in Basic Concepts to develop the examples shown here, by stretching and skewing, and by using other polygons and symmetrical repeats.

BASIC PLEATS
1. **Accordion Pleats**
1.1 Linear

2.1. Accordion Pleats

Accordion pleats are basic mountain-valley-mountain-valley pleats in which the folds are spaced equally in either a linear or rotational progression. The equality of spacing makes them particularly easy to fold and creates a satisfying, rhythmic repetition of light and shade.

Their simplicity also means that instead of focusing your creativity on the folding pattern, you can give your attention to the relationship between the pleats and the shape of the paper (or other material) from which they are made. The paper shapes shown here are just a few of the very many which, with a little imagination and experimentation, can be developed.

2.1.1 Linear

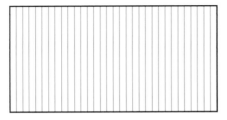

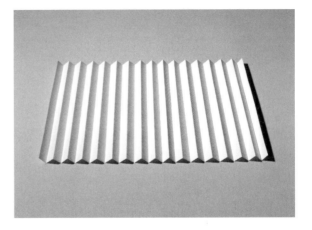

2.1.1 _ 1
This is the simplest example of an Accordion pleat – actually a recreation of the Linear Thirty-seconds example on page 19 of the Basic Concepts chapter.

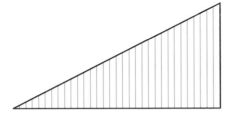

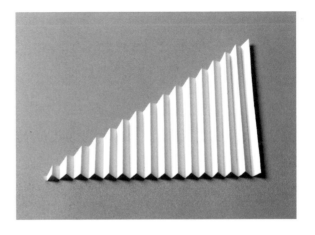

2.1.1 _ 2
A slope creates a complex zigzag edge when the pleats are gathered together. Try mirroring the shape to the left or below to create extra zigzag edges.

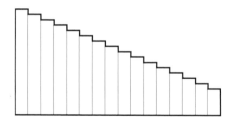

2.1.1 _ 3
Instead of a sloping edge, create a
stepped edge. Experiment widely with
the shape of the cut edge – it can become
extremely complex, perhaps even
figurative or typographic.

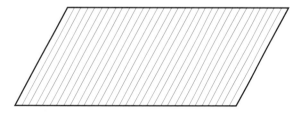

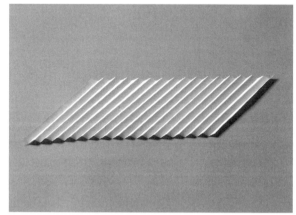

2.1.1 _ 4
A basic rectangle may be skewed to create
a parallelogram (see page 48). Experiment
with the angle of skew and the spacing of
the pleats to create different effects.

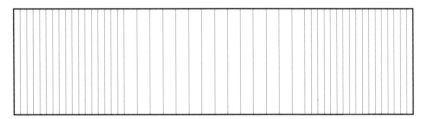

2.1.1 _ 5
Accordion pleats, although defined as regularly spaced, can nevertheless be grouped together in a sequence of spacings. In this example, the larger pleats in the centre are twice the size of the flanking pleats, though a great number of other patterns could be devised.

2.1.2   Rotational

2.1.2 _ 1
This basic rotational Accordion pleat divides a 360° circle into 16 equal angles, recreating the Rotational Sixteenths examples on pages 24–25.

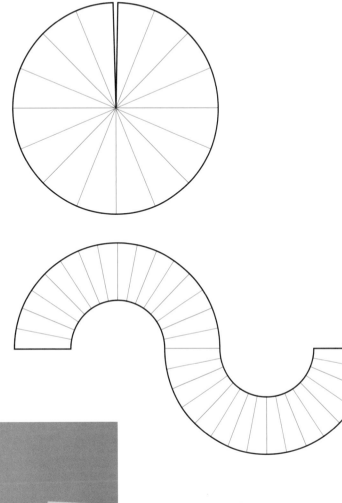

2.1.2 _ 2
Two semicircles are divided into sixteenths and joined end to end to create a letter 'S'. The pattern could continue infinitely.

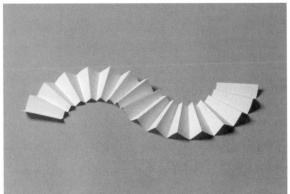

2.1.2 _ 2

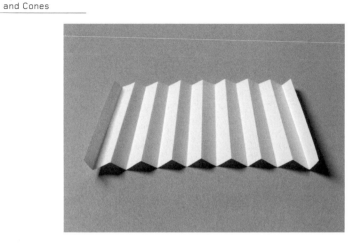

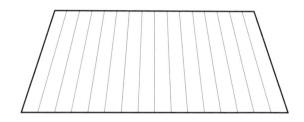

2.1.2 _ 3
Although the folds are rotational, no curved edges are used here. Note how all the folds would meet at an imaginary point. This example can be made quickly, without measuring any angles, using the Linear Sixteenths method (see pages 16–17).

2.1.3   Cylinders and Cones

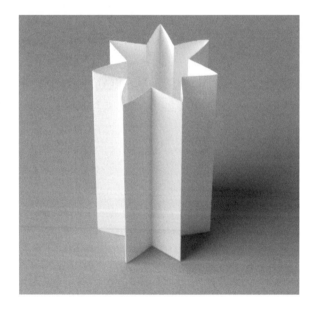

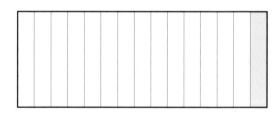

2.1.3 _ 1
A simple cylinder can be made by glueing one end of a line of Accordion pleats to the other. The example here shows the paper divided into sixteenths, but with one division cut off to leave an odd number – fifteenths. By creating an odd number of pleats, only one division needs to be glued and overlapped, not two divisions, so the paper will more readily assume a symmetrical star shape.

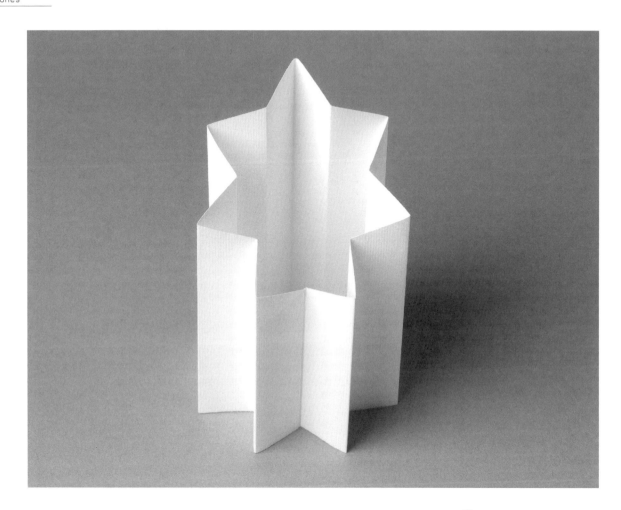

2.1.3 _ 2
The paper can also be cut to create an angle
rather than a level edge. It may be cut into
a silhouette that is much more complex than
the simple one shown here. The bottom edge
may also be cut. Note that as in the previous
example, the paper is divided into fifteenths,
not sixteenths, and only one division is
overlapped and glued.

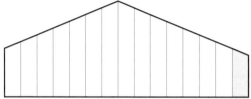

2.1.3 _ 3
A circle of paper is divided into
16 equal angles. The paper may
be divided into any even number
of angles, though the greater the
number, the messier the centre
point where all the folds meet will
become. The circular shape of the
paper may also be cut into a more
complex shape.

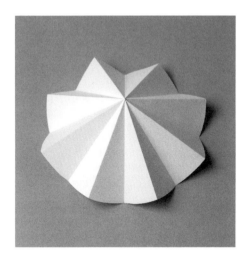
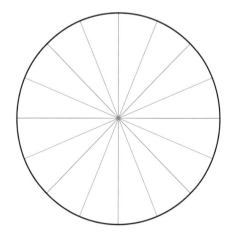

2.1.3 _ 4
A solid circle may also be cut as
a doughnut. Removing the centre
of the paper makes it easier to
add more folds and the shape has
much more flexibility. Removing
part of the 360° circle and glueing
the ends together converts a flat
zigzag into a cone.

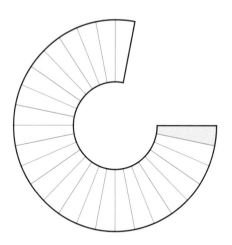

2.1.3 _ 5
Here, the paper is cut into the
shape of a pentagon and the 360°
angle is divided into ten equal
angles. For added interest, the
small cut-out pentagon in the
centre is rotated through 36°
in relation to the outer pentagon.

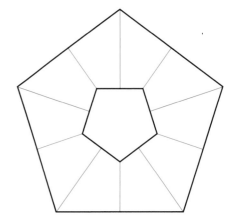

2.1.3 _ 6
When making doughnuts, the inner
cut-out shape need not be placed
symmetrically in the centre – it can
be moved off centre. The result is
subtle and somewhat curious.

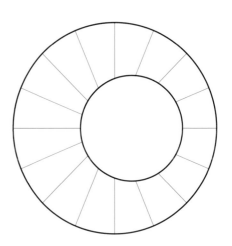

2.2.   Knife Pleats

Knife pleats are basic mountain-valley-mountain-valley... pleats placed in either a linear or rotational progression, but the spacing between the mountain-valley pairings differs from the spacing between the valley-mountain pairings.

Whereas the equality of the spacing of Accordion pleats makes them compress into a 3-D zigzag pile, the inequality of the spacing of Knife pleats means the pile will travel to the left or right, to create a 2-D surface. Being able to create a surface, plus the ability to define or change the inequality of the spacing between the folds, means Knife pleats are generally more useful — and so more commonly used — than Accordion pleats.

2.2.1. Linear

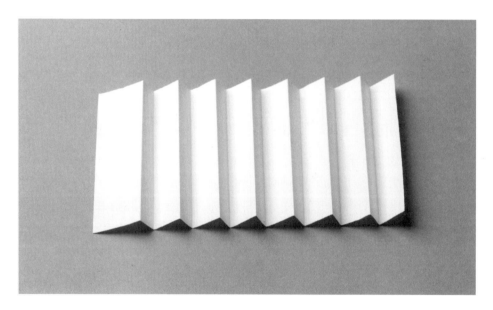

2.2.1 _ 1
A strip of paper is divided into eighths with mountain folds, then valley folds are placed one-third of the way between each mountain to create a 1-2-1-2-1-2 rhythm of Knife pleats across the paper. This may all be done by eye, or you may choose to measure the accurate placement of the valleys with a ruler.

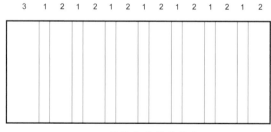

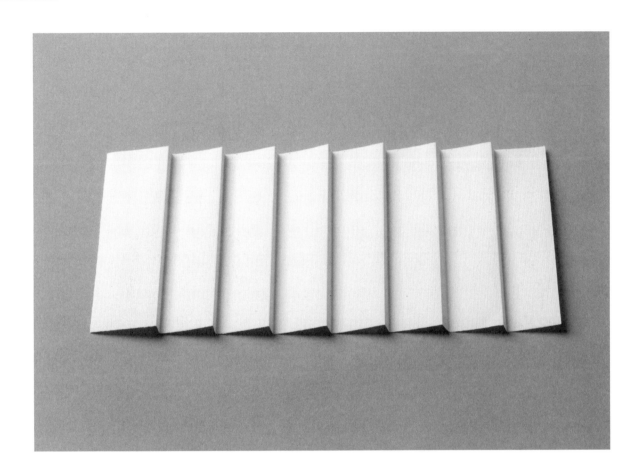

5 1 4 1 4 1 4 1 4 1 4 1 4 1 4

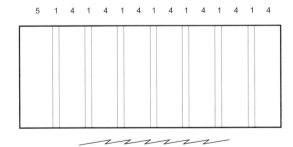

2.2.1 _ 2
Here, the mountain eighths have valley folds placed one-fifth of the way between them, to create a 1-4-1-4-1-4 rhythm across the paper. The effect is to space the Knife pleats farther apart than in the first example and to create an extended surface.

2.2.2.   **Rotational**

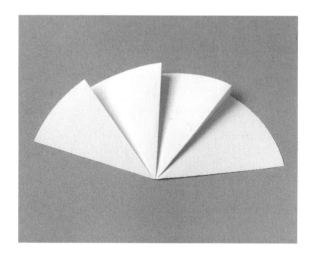

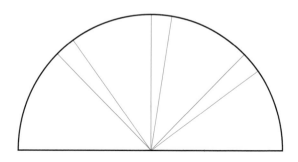

2.2.2 _ 1
Here, Knife pleats are arranged
around a semicircle. The shape
could also be a full circle or a
polygon, and the distance between
the mountain and valley folds that
make the pleat could also change.

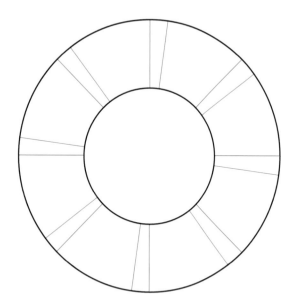

2.2.2 _ 2
This doughnut has eight Knife
pleats arranged around the rim.
Note how all the folds would
converge at the imaginary centre
and how the two folds in each pair
are not parallel to each other.

2.2.3.   Reflected

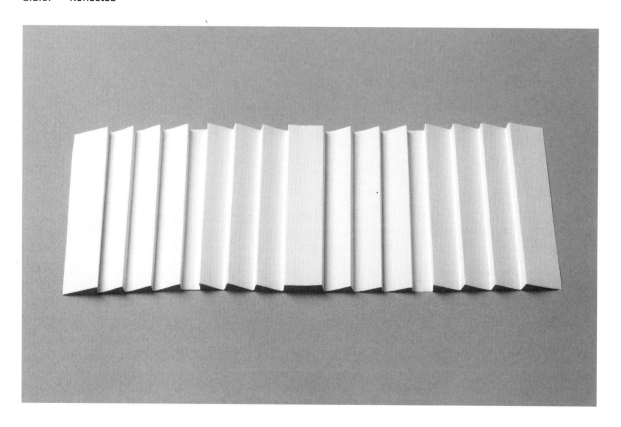

2.2.3 _ 1
A succession of Knife pleats can run in
a linear or rotational progression, then
be reflected (see 'Reflection' section
on page 35). In effect, the reflection
symmetry creates a mirror image, so that
a descending line of Knife pleats suddenly
ascends again (or vice versa). The example
shown here divides a paper strip into 17
equally spaced mountain folds. The valley
folds are one-quarter of the way between
each mountain. Many other reflected Knife
pleat patterns are possible.

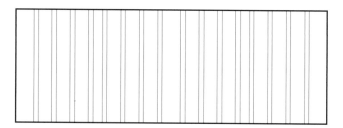

2.2.4.   Cylinders and Cones

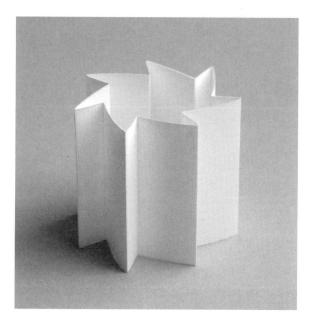

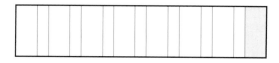

2.2.4 _ 1
A line of conventional Knife pleats can
create a cylinder if one end is glued
and joined to the other end. The top and
bottom edges can be cut into a variety of
complex shapes.

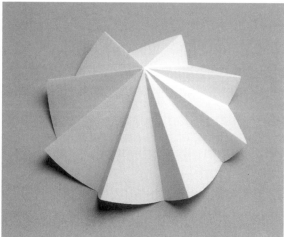

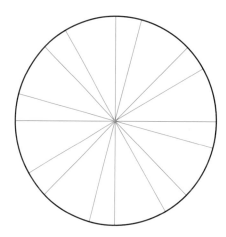

2.2.4 _ 2
Rotational Knife pleats will create a cone.
The greater the number of Knife pleats
and the closer they are together, the
more vertical the cone will be. Conversely,
fewer, narrower pleats will create a
relatively flat cone.

2.2.4 _ 3
A circular cone can instead be cut as
a straight-sided polygon, to create a
pyramid effect. Here, the top of the
pyramid has been removed. Pyramids can
be made with any number of sides, though
the more sides they have, the more they
will resemble a circular cone.

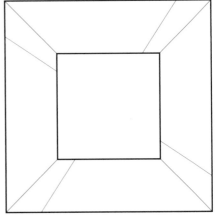

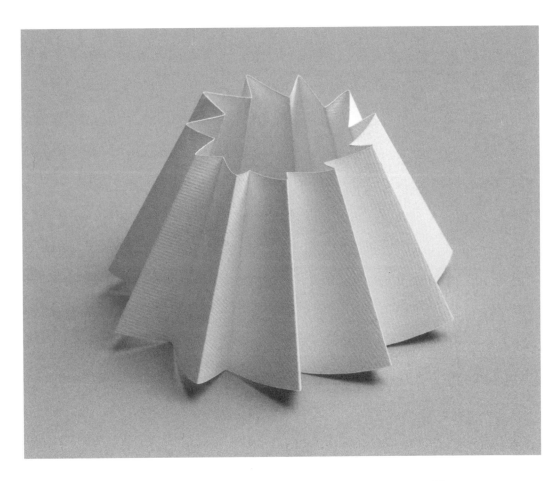

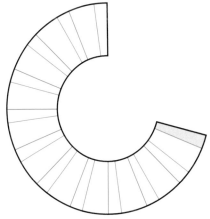

2.2.4 _ 4
The exact slope of a cone can be carefully
controlled by using not a full circle but
part of one, and by changing the number
and frequency of the Knife pleats. When
the ends are joined, cones of a precise
shape can be created.

2.3.   Box Pleats

Box pleats are a group of four folds, repeated in either a linear or rotational progression across a surface. The group begins with a simple Knife pleat valley-mountain pairing, which is then mirrored as a mountain-valley pairing, to create a valley-mountain-mountain-valley pattern which can be repeated across a surface.

Like Knife pleats, Box pleats have the ability to create a 2-D surface. However, whereas Knife pleats appear to ascend or descend across the surface like a flight of steps, Box pleats remain on a level and are thus less visually dynamic but more stable.

2.3.1. Linear

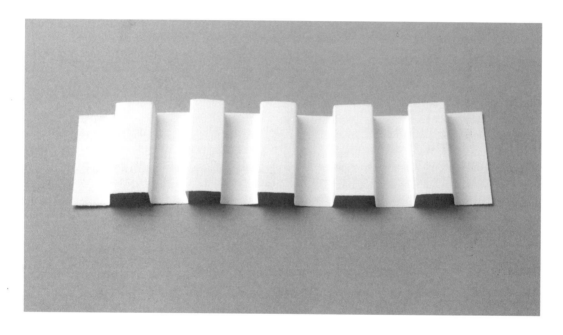

2.3.1 _ 1
This is the most basic Box pleat pattern, visually identical on the back. Note the alternating pairs of valley-mountain and mountain-valley pleats. The columns will nestle against each other when the paper is completely flat.

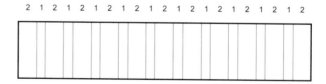

2 1 2 1 2 1 2 1 2 1 2 1 2 1 2 1 2 1 2 1 2

2.3.1 _ 2
The pattern of valley-mountain and
mountain-valley folds is identical to the
previous example, but the columns will
be separate when the paper is flattened.
They could be further separated. Note
that when the columns are separated,
the back is no longer identical to the front.

2 1 2 1   4   1 2 1   4   1 2 1   4   1 2 1 2 2

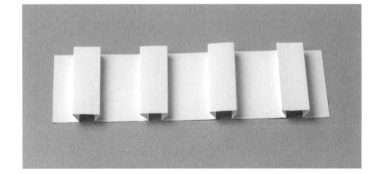

2.3.1 _ 3
In this example, the columns alternate
from the front to the back along the strip.
This separates the columns and also
makes the front and back visually identical.

2 1 2 1 2 1 2 1 2 1 2 1 2 1 2 1 2 1 2 1 2 1 2

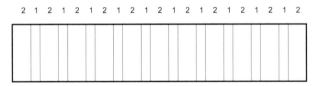

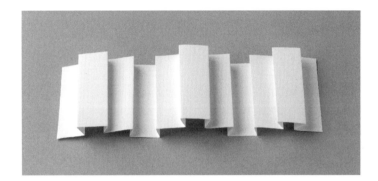

2.3.1 _ 4
Box pleats can be given an extra pleat
(or two, or more) to create very complex
surfaces. The possibilities of these extra
folds are immense and can be applied to
any of the examples in this section.

2 1 1 1 2 1 1 1 2 1 1 1 2 1 1 1 2 1 1 1 2 1 1 1 2

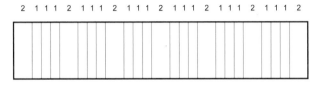

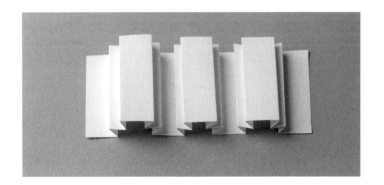

2.3.2.   Rotational

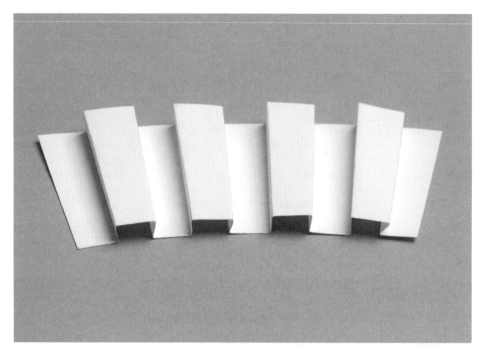

2.3.2 _ 1

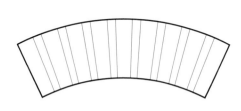

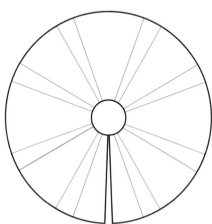

2.3.2 _ 1
Here, a basic Box pleat pattern is configured around the arc of a circle. Note how all the folds would extend to converge at the imaginary centre of the circle.

2.3.2 _ 2
Four large Box pleats are arranged around a full circle. The convergence of 16 folds in the centre could potentially be very unaesthetic, so a small circle has been cut away in the middle.

BASIC PLEATS
1.   **Box Pleats**
.2. Rotational

2.3.2 _ 2

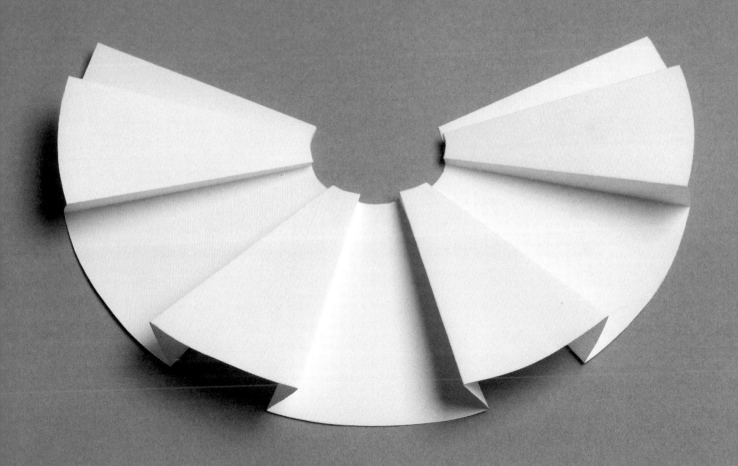

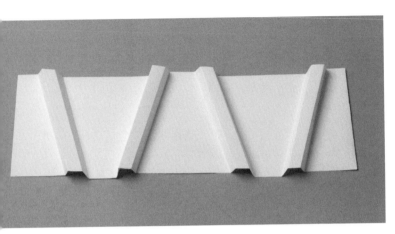

2.3.2 _ 3
Box pleats – or any other form of pleat –
need not be placed perpendicularly on
a strip. They may instead be placed at
an angle to create a less formal effect.
Here, the pattern uses reflection
symmetry (see page 35).

2.3.3. Cylinders and Cones

2.3.3 _ 1
Box pleats can create many cylindrical
and box shapes when one end of a strip
is glued to another. In most instances,
very different results will be created
depending on which surface of the paper –
the front or the back – is on the inside
or the outside of the strip. In this example,
two pieces are folded in the same way
but each is the other turned inside out.

2.3.3 _ 2
Circles or polygons (here, an octagon) can
be used to support patterns of Box pleats.
Try 'popping' a completed example inside
out; inverting the paper will make it look
very different. Thus, for every pattern of
folds that creates a conical or pyramidic
form, there are two possible 3-D forms,
each one the inverse of the other, like
the two pieces shown below. This is true
not only for Box pleating, but for any
pleat pattern.

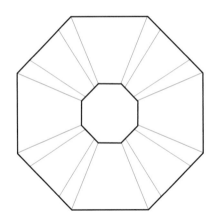

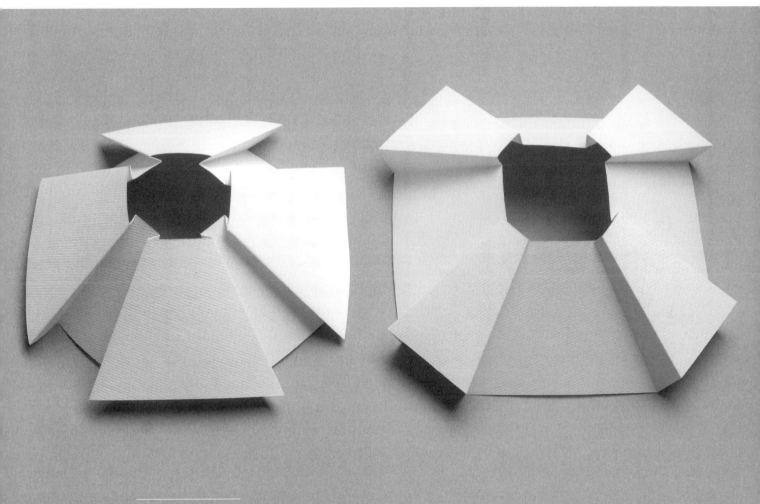

2.4.   Incremental Pleats

Incremental pleats are pleats in which the spacing between the folds
progressively increases or decreases. For example, the spacings could increase
10mm each time, from 10mm to 20mm, then 30mm, then 40mm, then 50mm and
so on, or perhaps the increase could be exponential, using a Fibonacci or
logarithmic sequence, for example. The progressions could also be irregular,
though this tends to create unaesthetic, confused-looking surfaces and forms.

Used well, Incremental pleats have the potential to create limitless pleated
patterns, particularly if combined with unusual material shapes and a creative
use of Accordion, Knife or Box pleat patterns. The pleat patterns in the following
chapter may also be made incrementally.

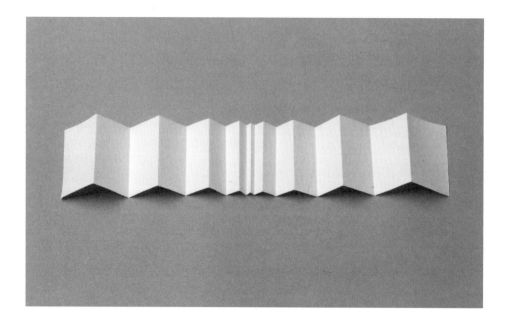

2.4 _ 1
Here, the distance between the pleats is
decreasing from the edge to the centre
and then is reflected to the opposite
edge. Complex topographic surfaces –
not necessarily symmetrical – can be
made in this way.

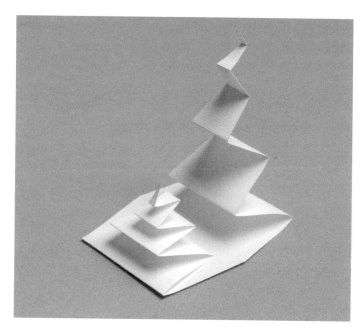

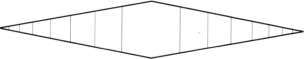

2.4 _ 2
Elaborate layering patterns are
achieved by reflecting a triangular
shape of incremental pleats.
The decorative effect could be
enhanced by using a sheet material
with a different colour or texture on
its two surfaces.

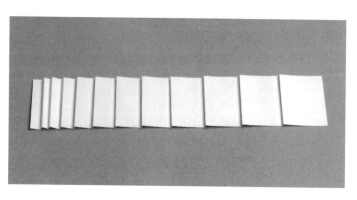

2.4 _ 3
These Knife pleats maintain a consistent
shape, but are spaced farther and farther
apart incrementally. The same effect could
be achieved with Box pleats.

3.   Other Pleats

The previous chapter introduced the four basic types of pleat and the next one shows how they can be used to create a huge array of surfaces and forms. This short chapter is transitional. It introduces concepts that are a little less basic, but which are still generic. As such, they deserve a chapter of their own.

Although short, this chapter could easily expand to become the longest in the book. A great number of variations can be derived from any set of basic techniques. The ones included here (Spiral pleats, Gathered pleats and Twisted pleats) are those which experience has shown to be the most useful and most versatile. However, in your own explorations you may well find other variations – even many others. As always, there is no substitute for picking up a sheet of paper and, using this book as a guide, beginning to fold and experiment.

3.1. Spiral Pleats

Spiral pleats and Box Spirals are generally simple to make and have essentially the same folding pattern: a strip of rectangles or trapeziums is divided by equally spaced mountain folds, then sloping parallel valley folds are placed diagonally between the mountains to connect them. The complete pattern of folds can be drawn in one continuous zigzag line.

3.1.1. Simple Spirals

A simple but beautiful spiralling pleat can be made by dividing a strip of paper into equal linear divisions with mountain folds (see pages 16–17), then folding a valley diagonal across each rectangle.

3.1.1 _ 1
The spiral here is laid horizontal, but suspended in moving air, it will revolve very gracefully. Collapsed flat, it will resemble a circular rosette. It can also be made from shapes other than a rectangular strip, such as a very long triangle or a very long rhombus.

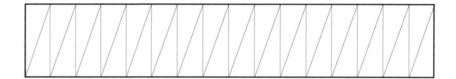

3.1.2.   Box Spirals

Box Spirals have the same folded configuration as the Simple Spiral on the preceding page, but are glued into box forms. This creates an overlapping of planes visually similar to the closed-up iris of a camera – but in 3-D, not 2-D – around the central point of the box. The structure resembles an hourglass.

The key to success is the precise control of the angle of the sloping valley fold, relative to the number of sides of the box. If the angle is too large, the box will be too tall; if too small, the box will be flat. It is worth taking as much time as possible to experiment with the angle, because even a few degrees can make a big difference to the final shape of the structure.

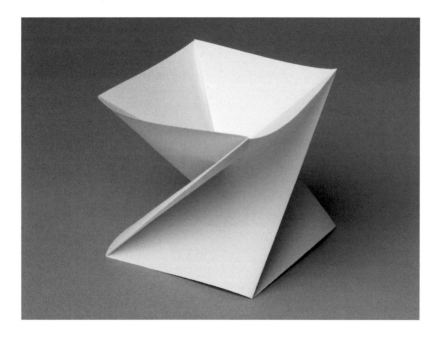

3.1.2 _ 1
This is a basic four-sided box form. Crease the mountains and valleys as shown, then apply glue to the tab and stick this tab to the opposite edge of the box. The box will assume its 'hourglass' form when the rectangular box form is twisted, as though closing the lid of a screw-top jar. There is a definite knack to the twisting, which becomes progressively more difficult as the number of sides increases.

3.1.2 _ 2
This is similar to the previous example,
except that a little of the top edge has
been cut away so that the valley and
mountain folds do not meet at the top
edge. The effect is to create an iris above
the centre point of the box and a more
decorative top edge.

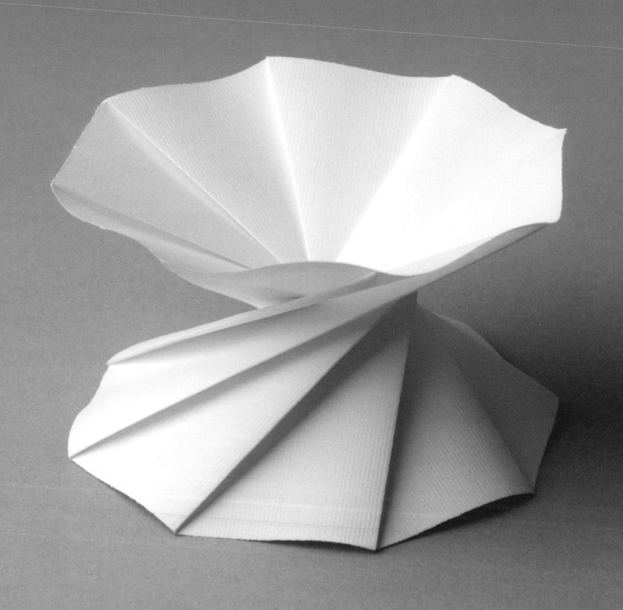

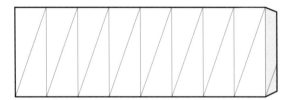

3.1.2 _ 3
The box can have any number of sides.
Here there are eight. The advantage of
a box with an even number of sides (such
as four, six or eight) is that it can be
pressed flat from left to right (or from
front to back) and erected instantly. Try
it – the transformation from 2-D to 3-D
is extraordinary! The angle of the sloping
valley fold is 70°. See photo opposite.

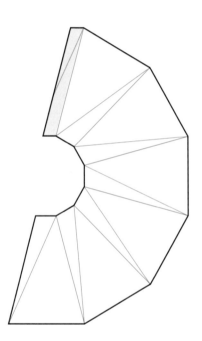

3.1.2 _ 4
Instead of dividing the paper into
rectangles with parallel mountain folds,
trapeziums may be created. In this
example, six trapeziums connect, with
their sides sloping at 75°. The valley folds
slope at 65° relative to the bottom edge of
each trapezium. The effect is to create a
form that tapers towards the top.

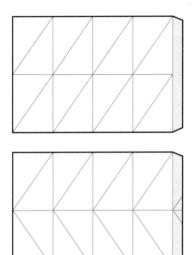

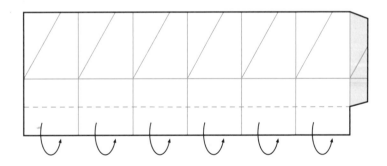

3.1.2 _ 5
Box Spirals can be stacked one on another
many times, to create towers of great
strength. Here, one four-sided box is
stacked on another, but in two different
ways. In the first example, the two boxes
use sloping valleys placed on the same
diagonal; in the second example, the
two boxes use sloping valleys placed on
different diagonals. When connecting
boxes together, either example may
be used.

3.1.2 _ 6
Box Spirals may be used to create
decorative lids. This lid is six-sided and
the sloping valley is at an angle of 60°
to the horizontal. A 3-D 'hourglass' lid
may be created by increasing the angle
to 61°, 62° etc. The greater the number
of degrees, the taller the lid will become.
Fold the bottom edge behind along the
dotted line. This will give extra strength
to the sides of the lid. See photo opposite.

3.2.   Gathered Pleats

Linear or rotational pleats may be left open, or may be gathered together
at one or both edges. When gathered together, many new forms and relief
surfaces become possible.

There are many ways to hold Gathered pleats together. The examples
described here use paper glue-tabs, but you could find other ways, such as
binding, riveting, stitching or stapling, depending on your choice of material(s).
As always, although the book presents paper and folding in visually 'pure'
ways, you are encouraged to be as disrespectful as you wish, in order to
make a design work for you.

3.2.1 Accordion Pleats

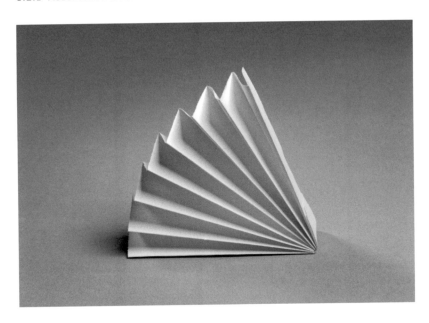

3.2.1 _ 1
This is a repeat of 1.1.1.six _ 11 (see
page 17), but with the addition of a glue
tab. Concertina all the pleats tightly
together, apply adhesive to the tab and
glue it to the pleat at the far end of the
concertina. This will gather one edge of
the concertina together to create a form
resembling a fan.

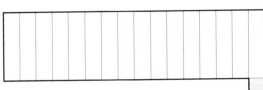

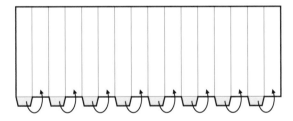

3.2.1 _ 2
Whereas one edge of the concertina was
fully closed in the previous example, here
just one row of corners is held together
along a concertinaed edge. This enables
the flat fan to become a 3-D cone. Apply
adhesive to the tabs, then concertina the
pleat. Glue each tab on to the next pleat,
thus half closing the concertinaed edge.

3.2.1 _ 3
The techniques described in the previous
two examples may also be used at the
other concertinaed edge of the pleats,
thus closing or half closing both edges.
An additional fold across the middle of
the paper will keep the pleats open at
the midpoint.

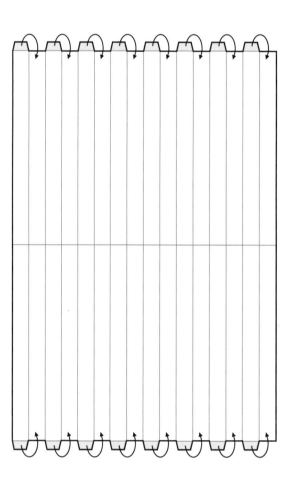

3.2.2. Knife Pleats

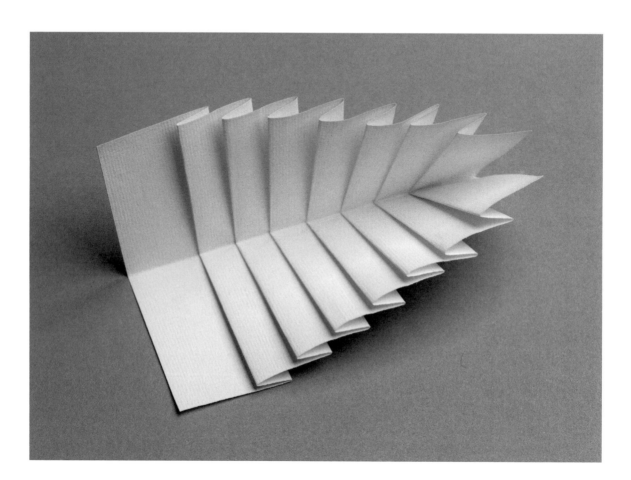

3.2.2 _ 1
This is a repeat of 2.2.1 _ 1 (see page 64), but with an additional valley fold across the middle, made after the Knife pleats have been folded. This additional fold gathers the pleats together along the midpoint, but allows the edges to open. The effect is to create a form closed at one end and progressively more open towards the other.

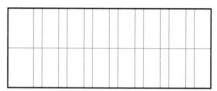

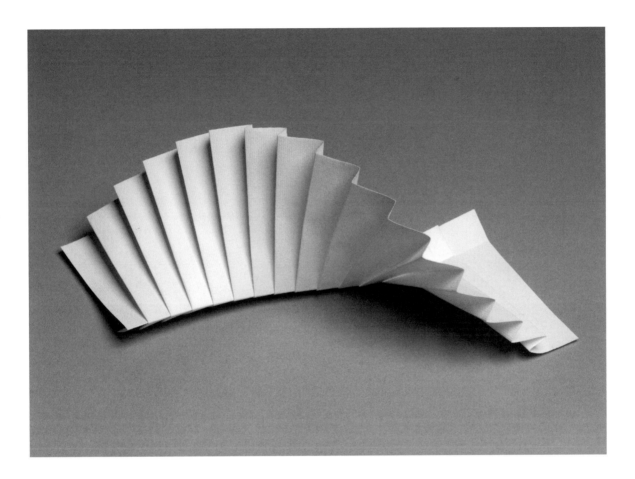

3.2.2 _ 2
Here, a line of 16 Knife pleats is
gathered along one edge. This allows
the ungathered edge to splay open
and spiral around the gathered edge,
to create a form resembling a spiral
staircase. Instead of being folded,
the edge could be closed with stitches,
tape, staples, etc.

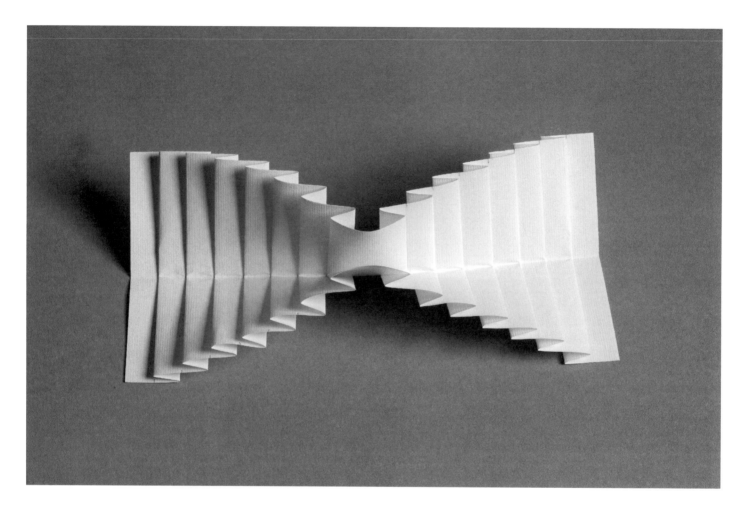

3.2.2 _ 3
Seven Knife pleats on the left of the strip
are mirrored on the right, to create a
form which is two examples of 3.2.2 _ 1
(see page 94) placed back to back.
The effect is to make a form that is open at
the left and right, but closed in the middle.
If more mirror fold patterns were created
on an extended strip, the pleated pattern
would open and close repeatedly.

3.2.2 _ 4
Seven Knife pleats on the left are
mirrored on the right, gathered together
with a long mountain fold near the top
edge. This is effectively half of the
previous example, but it is a relief
surface not a 3-D form.

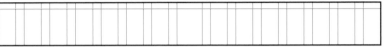

3.3.   Twisted Pleats

Twisted pleats are an excellent way to create visual interest on a flat surface. They can look a little stressed if made in paper or another stiff material, but made in something soft, such as fabric, they look much more relaxed and natural. For this reason, they are much used in apparel and in fashion accessories (bags, belts, hats, shoes, etc).

The examples here show the basic ways in which Twisted pleats can be used but, as always, you are encouraged to experiment widely, especially with reference to the Basic Concepts and Basic Pleats chapters.

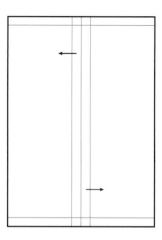

3.3 _ 1
This is the basic technique. Make three folds down the centre, so that the pleat stands upright like a shallow tennis net. Open the paper. Make and unfold horizontal mountain folds near the top and bottom edges. Reform the net. Flatten it to the left side at the top, trapping it flat with the horizontal fold. At the bottom, flatten it to the right side, trapping it flat with the horizontal fold. Instead of making horizontal folds to trap the pleat flat, you may use stitches, rivets, staples, etc.

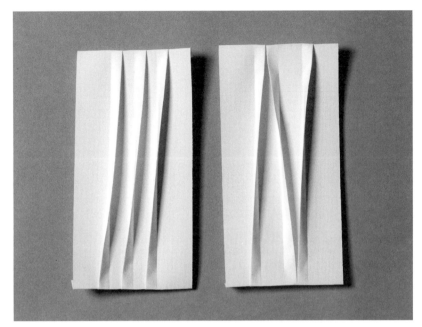

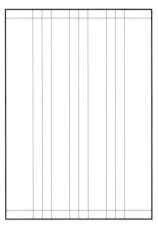

3.3 _ 2
A Linear progression of Twisted pleats can follow one of two patterns. Either all the pleats can twist in the same direction, or each pleat can be twisted in the opposite direction to its immediate neighbours. The photograph shows an example of each.

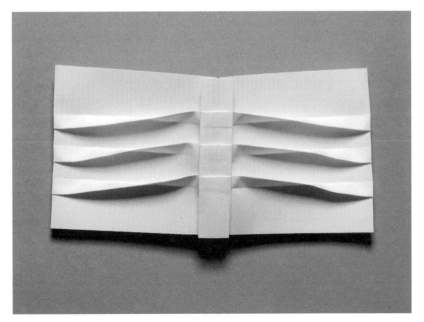

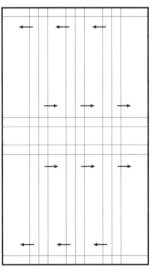

3.3 _ 3
The addition of a Box pleat (see page 72) can further trap the pleats so that they can be twisted, be held flat by the Box pleat and then be twisted back. If the material is long enough, a pleat may be twisted back and forth many times along its length. Instead of using Box pleats, you can use stitches, rivets, staples, etc. to secure the pleats.

4.   V-pleats

This chapter has the potential to turn the technique of pleating into an extreme sport. The concepts it presents can be developed to ever greater levels of difficulty, to create relief surfaces and 3-D forms of impressive complexity.

But do not panic! Remarkable results can be achieved with even the simplest V-pleating. This is because almost all V-pleats are dynamic: they have the ability to make a surface expand and contract, and bend and twist in many directions. They have no fixed form, permitting movement in a wide variety of ways, depending on the placement of the folds.

V-pleats are fascinating to explore, and this exploration is potentially addictive. The pursuit of ever more complex patterns, with more folds, more repetitions and increasingly complex geometry, can be very seductive, consuming unnecessary design time with little result. It is easy to become lost in the labyrinth of technical possibilities, exploring simply for the sake of it. If you have time to explore, then this origami nirvana is enviable. But if your time is limited, it is crucial to be clear about what you wish to achieve.

4.1. Basic V-pleats

V-pleats are characterized by their distinctive 'V' shape, in which three mountain folds and one valley fold (or one mountain fold and three valley folds) meet at a node. A linear progression of V-pleats can extend infinitely across a sheet. In most instances, all the folds can be manipulated simultaneously so that the paper can concertina into a small, flat shape.

4.1 _ 1
This is the most basic V-pleat. Note the symmetry of the crease pattern and the precise configuration of mountains and valleys. The central line – called the 'line of symmetry' – may be placed anywhere on the sheet, but the V-folds must be placed symmetrically to each side of the line.

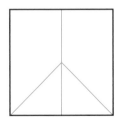 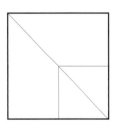

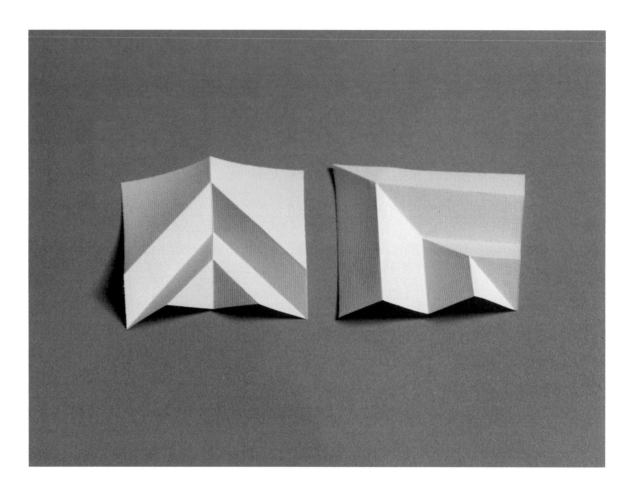

4.1 _ 2
V-pleats need not be made singularly,
but may progress infinitely along the
line of symmetry. The Vs must alternate
mountain-valley-mountain-valley along the
line. Note, too, how the line of symmetry
alternates between mountain and valley
between successive pleats.

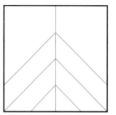
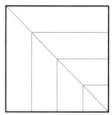

4.2.   Making by Hand

V-pleats create complex crease patterns of many small mountain and valley
folds. These patterns may be drawn in a computer, then printed out and folded,
or drawn directly on the sheet with geometry equipment, but it is often much
easier and quicker to make them by hand. This is surprisingly easy, though,
as usual, you will need to extrapolate the method given here into other crease
patterns of your own design.

4.2 _ 1
Fold a square along a diagonal.
Open the paper and turn the fold inside
out so that it may fold as a mountain
or a valley, without preference. This is
called a 'universal' fold. See page 8
for a more detailed explanation of
how to make a universal fold.

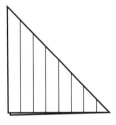

4.2 _ 2
Fold the paper in either direction along
the diagonal, then divide this triangle into
eighths through both layers, making each
crease a universal fold.

4.2 _ 3
This is the completed crease pattern.
Whatever the design of the pattern,
it is always most helpful to make all the
folds universal so that the paper will
collapse easily.

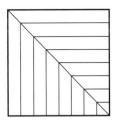

How to Collapse the Creased Paper

4.2 _ 4
Hold the paper as shown –
symmetrically, with thumbs
on the front and fingers
behind, and the longest
V-fold across the top of
the paper. Use your fingers
and thumbs to help the
longest upturned V become
a mountain fold.

4.2 _ 5
The V-fold below the
mountain V just formed
should now be creased
as a valley. Again, work
front and back on the
paper, using your fingers
and thumbs to create the
valley fold.

4.2 _ 6
Continue to make more
V-folds, alternating them
mountain-valley-mountain-
valley. They will become
progressively shorter and
shorter. Keep the folded
Vs gathered between your
fingers and thumbs; never
allow the paper to
become flat.

4.2 _ 7
The folds will collapse
to create a flat stick.

4.2 _ 8
The flat stick can be
pulled open to reveal
the V-folds inside.

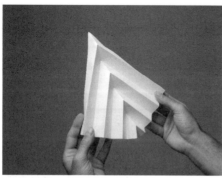

4.3. Variations

The two basic elements of V-pleating – the line of symmetry and the V-pleats themselves – can be taken through an extraordinary array of variations without introducing anything fundamentally new. Here are four ways in which the basic V-pleat can be developed. Most of these examples can be made by hand, as described on pages 105–107.

4.3.1. Moving the Line of Symmetry

The obvious location for a line of symmetry is on a line of symmetry within the sheet. However, the line can be placed anywhere, at the designer's discretion. Here are three ideas.

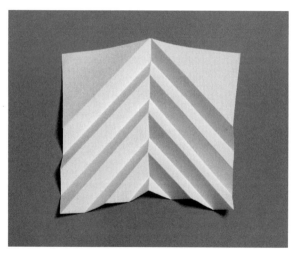

4.3.1 _ 1
This is the most basic location, along the vertical line of symmetry.

4.3.1 _ 2
Here, the line of symmetry is moved to the left, so that when the V-pleats are made, the two lines of pleats at each side of the V are of unequal length.

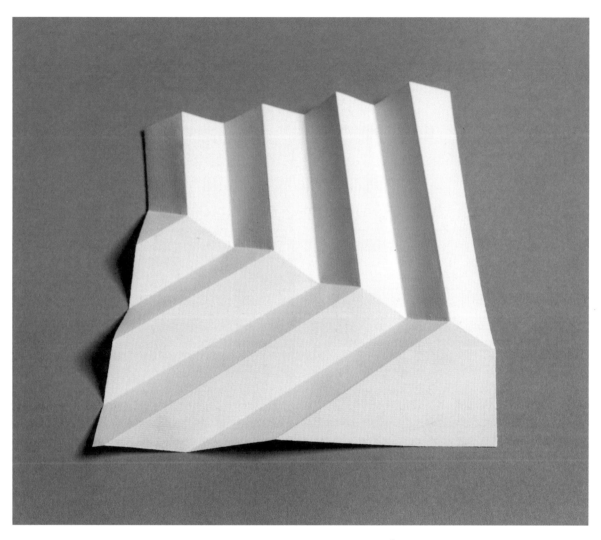

4.3.1 _ 3
In this example, the line of symmetry is
located more or less randomly on the
sheet. It is instructive to repeat this
exercise on a dozen or more sheets,
deliberately placing the line of symmetry
in different places each time.

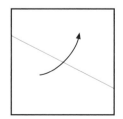 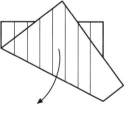 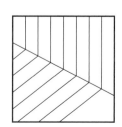

4.3.2.   Changing the Angle of the V-pleats

So far, almost all the examples given have been with the V-pleats at 45° to the line of symmetry. However, the angle can be anything between a few degrees more than 0° and a few degrees less than 90°, and can even change along the line.

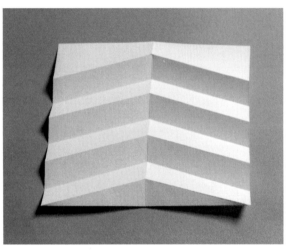

4.3.2 _ 1
Here the angle is approximately 75°. When all the pleats are collapsed, the sheet will become much smaller than it would be if the pleats were placed at a tighter angle.

4.3.2 _ 2
Here, the angle is approximately 30°. Compare this example with the previous one. A simple change of angle makes a radical difference to the collapsed form.

4.3.2 _ 3
The angles of the V-pleats may change
along the line of symmetry. There are,
however, certain limitations to this
system, since it will not always permit the
sheet to collapse totally flat. As always,
experimentation will help you separate
the possible from the impossible.

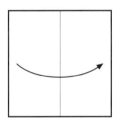 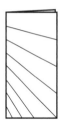 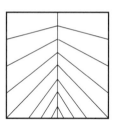

4.3.3.   Breaking Symmetry

So far, the angle of a V-pleat on one side of the line of symmetry has been mirrored on the other side, so the folding patterns have been symmetrical. However, symmetry is optional. The Japanese origami master Toshikazu Kawasaki developed what is known as the Kawasaki Theorem, which permits V-pleat asymmetry if certain other conditions are met.

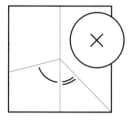

4.3.3 _ 1
In this basic example, the paper will fold flat in half along the V-pleat because the two marked angles are equal. The crease pattern is symmetrical.

4.3.3 _ 2
Here, the same marked angles on the two sides of the line of symmetry are unequal. Although this crease pattern can of course be folded, the paper will not collapse flat.

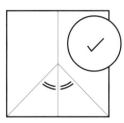

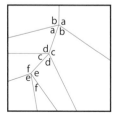

4.3.3 _ 3
In order for paper to collapse flat with an asymmetric crease pattern, the Kawasaki Theorem states that there must be an even number of angles around the node (four, six, eight, etc.) and alternate angles must total 180°. Thus, a + a = b + b = 180°. Note that for this formula to work, the line of symmetry must change direction through the node.

4.3.3 _ 4
The formula will work for any number of V-pleats along a line of symmetry. Some care must be taken with the positioning of the folds so that the result does not look like a chaotic doodle (unless that is what you want, of course). a + a = b + b = c + c = d + d = e + e = f + f = 180°.

4.3.4.   Coexisting Vs

Separate lines of V-pleats can exist independently on the same sheet, though some care must be taken to place them accurately so that they do not touch or interfere with each other. Separate lines may also be built one on another in a succession of V-pleat generations, to create a crease pattern somewhat resembling the forking of a tree trunk into ever smaller branches.

4.3.4 _ 1
Here, four separate lines of V-pleats recede into the corners, leaving the edges and centre unpleated. The same crease pattern can be tried with other polygons.

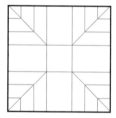

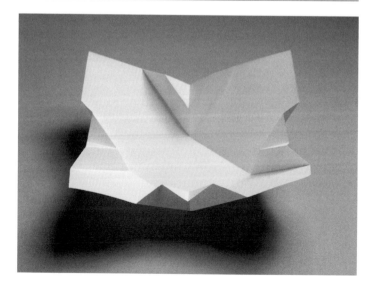

4.3.4 _ 2
Similarly, four lines of V-pleats recede to the edges, leaving the diagonals and centre unpleated.

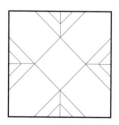

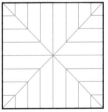

4.3.4 _ 3
The four lines of V-pleats meet at the
centre point of the sheet, enabling the
final form to take two entirely different
forms – each is the other 'popped' inside
out (inverted).

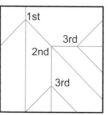

4.3.4 _ 4
First, the 1st generation V-pleat is made
near the top-left corner of the sheet.
Then, the 2nd generation pleat is made near
the centre, after which two 3rd generation
pleats are made. Other generations may
be added. Any of the variations discussed
above may be used with this generations
idea. The sheet will collapse to create a
flat stick.

4.4.   Multiple V's

This is the point in the chapter when making V-pleats can become an extreme sport. The V-pleats made on pages 103–106 will now duplicate themselves sideways, so that a V-form becomes a W or M. They are connected by new lines of symmetry, arranged in linear, radial or random patterns. In the example shown here (4.4.1 _ 1), three lines of symmetry connect two lines of Vs to create an M-form. As before, these Multiple Vs will collapse flat if the conditions of the Kawasaki Theorem are observed.

4.4.1 _ 1

4.4.2.   Making by Hand

Like the simple V-pleats earlier in the chapter, Multiple Vs may also be folded by hand. The method is fundamentally the same, though it entails more work and a greater commitment to accuracy.

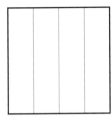

4.4.2 _ 1
Fold the sheet into quarters. It will be helpful if these are made as universal folds (see page 105).

4.4.2 _ 2
Create angled folds through all four layers of the paper, again as universal folds.

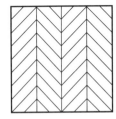

4.4.2 _ 3
Open the paper. This is the completed crease pattern.

How to Collapse the Creased Paper

4.4.2 _ 4
Hold the paper in the air, symmetrically, with thumbs on the front and fingers on the back. Select an M-fold approximately in the middle of the paper. Using your fingers and thumbs, pop and press the creases to make a mountain M from left to right across the paper, while at the same time defining the three vertical folds (the lines of symmetry) as mountains or valleys. Do not allow the paper to flatten – this will lose all the newly made folds.

4.4.2 _ 5
Repeat, but this time make a valley M. Note that the three vertical lines of symmetry below the valley M must be allowed to swap from valley to mountain and from mountain to valley. All three folds are the opposite to the folds seen in the previous step.

4.4.2 _ 6
Continue to make successive lines of M-pleats that alternate mountain-valley-mountain-valley down the paper to the bottom edge.

4.4.2 _ 7
Similarly, now make the remaining M-pleats, working from the first M-pleat made up to the top edge of the paper.

4.4.2 _ 8
When all the folds have been made, collapse the paper into a narrow stick and press it flat with some force in order to sharpen all the folds.

4.4.2 _ 9
The stick can be pulled
open to reveal the
M-pleats inside.

4.4.3.   Variations

The folding of several lines of symmetry on to which angled folds are superimposed can take many forms. Here are examples to make by hand, which explore the three most basic themes. As before, it is most helpful to fold all the creases as universal folds.

4.4.3.1 Radial

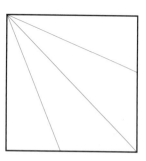

4.4.3.1 _ 1
Divide the corner into four
equal angles of 22.5°.

4.4.3.1 _ 2
Place three (or more)
angled folds across
the paper.

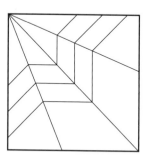

4.4.3.1 _ 3
Open the paper and
collapse the folds as
described on page 118.
See photo opposite.

4.4.3.2. Parallel, but Unequal

4.4.3.2 _ 3

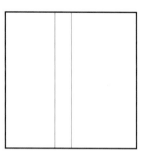

4.4.3.2 _ 1
Make two parallel lines of
symmetry folds.

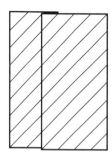

4.4.3.2 _ 2
Make a progression of
angled folds across
the paper.

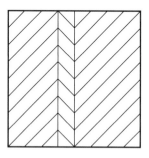

4.4.3.2 _ 3
Open the paper and
collapse the folds as
described on page 118.

4.4.3.3 Random Lines of Symmetry

4.4.3.3 _ 3

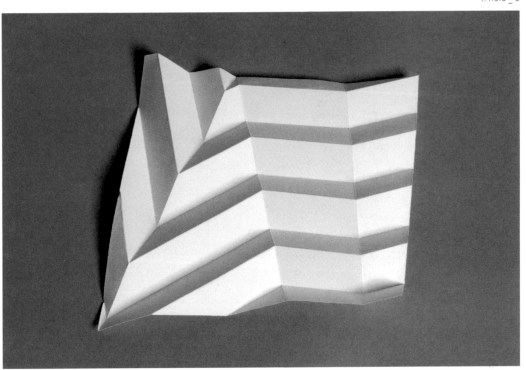

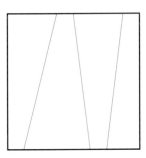

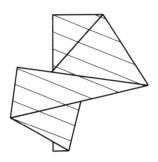

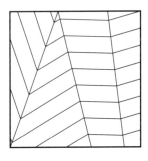

4.4.3.3 _ 1
The lines of symmetry can
be placed randomly (or
seemingly so) on the sheet.

4.4.3.3 _ 2
Take care to place the
angled lines in such a way
that they do not cross
a line of symmetry at an
angle approaching 0°
or 90°. It can take
a few attempts to do
this correctly.

4.4.3.3 _ 3
Open the paper and
collapse the folds as
described on page 118.

4.5.   Grid Vs

Multiple V's can have many more lines of symmetry than the two or three described earlier, which creates the effect of a grid of repeated Vs. The simplest way to achieve this effect is to first fold the grid by hand, then collapse the paper along only some of the folds to create countless V-pleats variations. The grid needs to be folded with accuracy.

4.5.1. Making by Hand

The method described here divides the sheet diagonally into 32 and horizontally into 16. For a simpler effect, divide the paper diagonally into 16 and horizontally into 8.

4.5.1 _ 1
Using the method described on page 27, divide the paper into 32 along a diagonal. The folds may be left as mountain-valley pleats, or you may convert all of them to universal folds (see page 105).

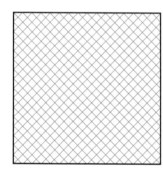

4.5.1 _ 2
Similarly, divide the other diagonal into 32.

4.5.1 _ 3
Now divide the paper into vertical sixteenths from left to right. Convert these folds to universal folds. You may also add sixteenths as horizontal folds, though this is not essential. This is the completed grid, from which many Multiple V designs can be created. The photo opposite shows the maximum number of Vs that can be created from the crease pattern made on this page. See also page 128.

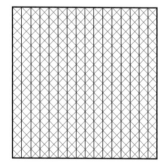

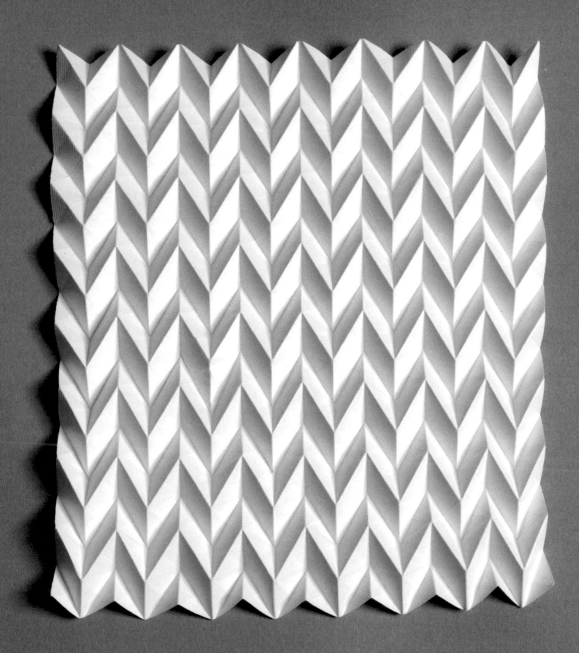

How to Collapse the Creased Paper

4.5.1 _ 4
Crease the 15 vertical lines of symmetry
to make simple accordion pleats. Hold the
creased paper symmetrically as shown,
with thumbs on the front and fingers on
the back.

4.5.1 _ 5
Use your fingers and thumbs to pop and press
a double row of zigzags. The upper line is a
mountain zigzag; the lower line is a valley zigzag.
Use existing mountain and valley folds to find
these folds. You do not need to invent any new
folds! Work across the paper from edge to edge,
opening only the part of the paper where you are
working. The remainder of the paper can
be concertinaed closed.

4.5.1 _ 6
This is the double row of zigzags, completed.
It can take some time to acquire the knack of
how to make them.

4.5.1 _ 7
Continue to make these double rows of
zigzags until you reach the bottom edge
of the paper.

4.5.1 _ 8
Now go back to the middle of the paper
and work upwards, creating more double
rows of zigzags until the top edge of the
paper is reached.

4.5.1 _ 9
Collapse the paper into a very narrow,
thick stick. Press it flat to sharpen all
the folds.

4.5.1 _ 10
Pull open the stick to reveal the zigzags
inside. Pour yourself a drink.

4.5.2. Variations

Here are just a very few of the many variations that can be made by selecting some or all of the lines of symmetry and some or all of the V-pleats. All the creases already exist on the grid.

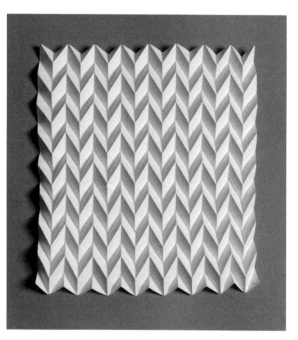

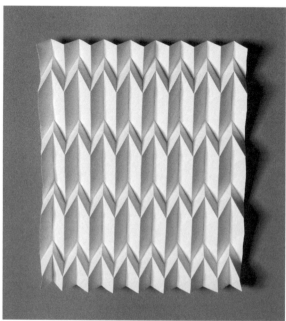

4.5.2 _ 1
This is the full Multiple V grid, using all the lines of symmetry and all the V-pleats. It becomes an extraordinarily flexible parabolic surface.

4.5.2 _ 2
Some of the V-pleats may be omitted to create a pattern that is less dense.

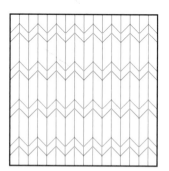

4.5.2 _ 3
Alternatively, some of the
lines of symmetry may be
omitted, so that in places
the V-pleats may extend
in length.

4.6   Cylindrical Vs

The relief surfaces of V-pleats will flex in many directions. One obvious way to flex them is to bend the surface into a cylinder, then glue the ends together to make the cylinder permanent. Here are two simple examples, though you could design many others. You will find that these designs become very flexible, almost like toys.

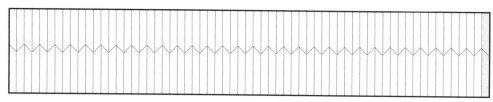

4.6 _ 1
This rectangle is proportioned approximately
6 x 1 and is divided into 64.
One division is
cut off, so that when the paper is folded and
bent into a cylinder, there is a glued overlap
of just one division. The long V-pleat can be
made from a pre-folded grid of diagonals,
or drawn and folded by hand.

Flexing by Hand

This sequence of photographs shows a few of the many different positions into which the cylinder can be flexed. With a little practice, it can be made to move continuously in the hand!

4.6 _ 2   4.6 _ 3   4.6 _ 4

4.6 _ 5
The Cylindrical V from the facing
page in its resting position.

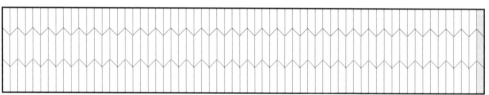

4.6 _ 6
This is similar in many respects to the
previous example, except that there are
now two lines of V-pleats that divide the
sheet into approximate thirds. The extra
pleated section allows for more play and
for flexed forms of greater intricacy.
A more complex version, with four lines
of V-pleats, is used for the 19th-century
parlour entertainment, 'Troublewit'.
This version will bend and flex to make
many recognizable objects. Look for details
online, or in books on traditional magic.

4.7.   Complex Surfaces

The folded grid can be used to create many extraordinary surfaces that are even more complex than the relatively simple V-pleat ones made in the two previous sections. There are no limits here, other than your time, technical prowess and imagination.

An interesting alternative to the 45° diagonal grid used here is a grid of 60° diagonals, which cover the paper with equilateral triangles. No examples are given here – the possibilities of this grid are left as a challenge.

Grids of 45° and 60° create what origami enthusiasts call 'tessellations'. Entering 'origami tessellations' into an online search engine or photo site will bring up many remarkable examples of geometric folding.

4.7 _ 1

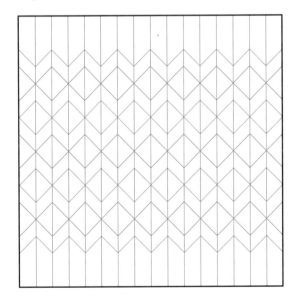

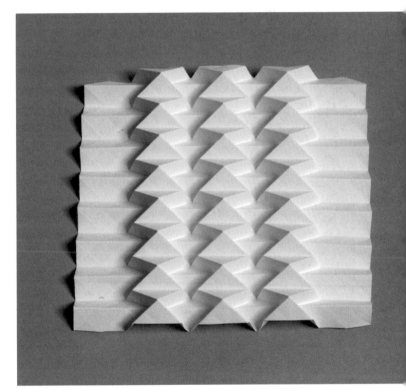

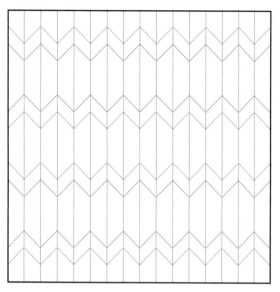

4.7 _ 2

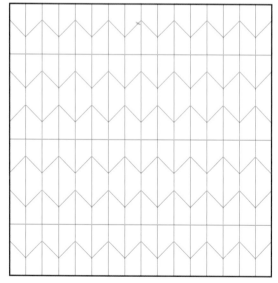

4.7 _ 3

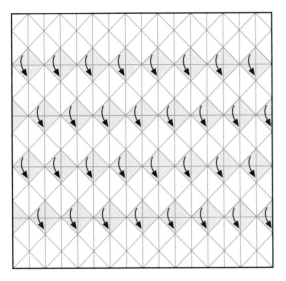

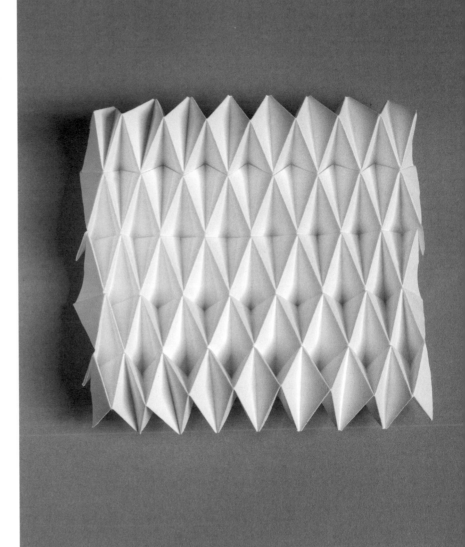

4.7 _ 4
The grey diamonds shown in the diagram
are folded in half so that each top corner
touches each bottom corner, closing them
up. The paper has also been trimmed from
a 16 x 16 grid to a 16 x 15 grid, solely to
make the folded surface, top and bottom,
appear more balanced.

5.   Spans & Parabolas

This final chapter about pleats shows how a sheet can be used to create spans and parabolas that touch the ground along an edge or at a corner, and then, through a progression of folded angles, rise upwards, across and down to create a form which resembles a canopy, roof or span.

Whereas most folded spans are 'simple curves' which curve in only one direction, like a cylinder, a folded parabola is a 'complex curve' which curves in two directions, like a sphere. Of course, the apparent curves of a folded span or parabola are purely illusory, since all the folded edges are straight and the planes between them are flat.

The natural curvature of the folded sheet in these span and parabolic forms gives them great strength, although they are usually only one layer thick. The occurrence of many triangles bounded by folds adds further to the strength of the structures (the triangle is the strongest and most stable of all polygons). Intriguingly, although they display 100 per cent of the surface area of the sheet, many of these structures can be concertinaed flat into a narrow stick.

5.1. X-form Spans

These spans are made from a repeated pattern of folds which resemble an X. In each case, the crease pattern is the same, but it is compressed or stretched to change the geometry of the span, and hence its curvature. Each span is a section of a cylinder.

5.1 _ 1
This is the basic X-form on a square sheet, made by dividing the paper horizontally and diagonally into eighths (see pages 16–17 and 27). For the span to form, the centre point of every X must be convex – that is, rise up towards you. See photo opposite.

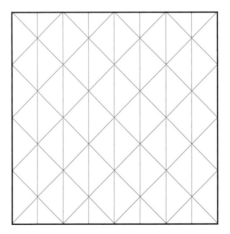

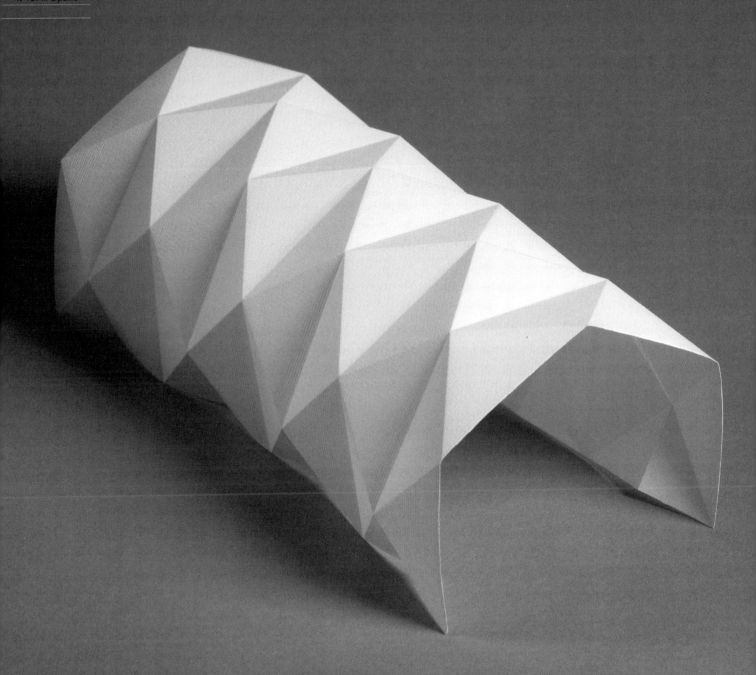

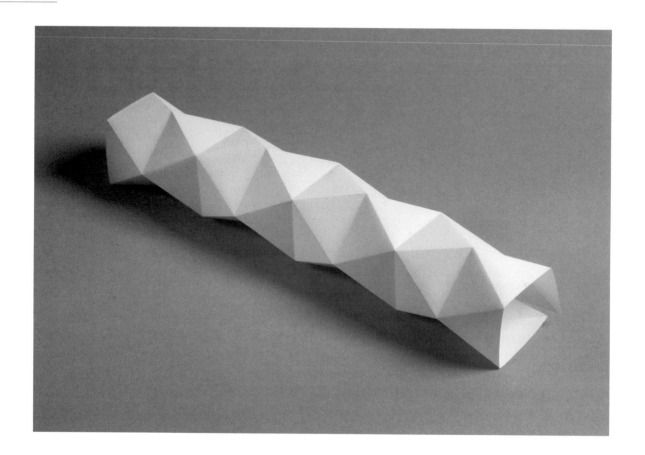

5.1 _ 2
The crease pattern here is the same as
in 5.1 _ 1, but is stretched horizontally so
that the angle between the strokes of each
X is 60°, not 90° as before. The result is
to make a span that curls so quickly back
on itself that it hardly makes a span at all;
rather, it is a narrow, faceted tube.

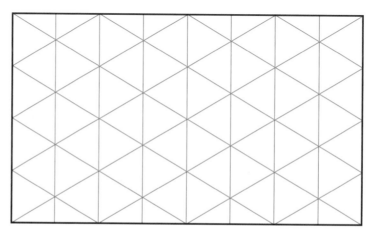

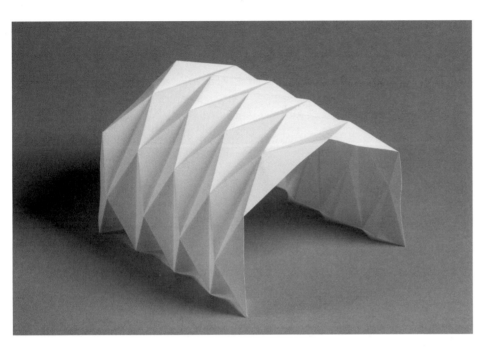

5.1 _ 3
By stretching the 5.1 _ 1 crease pattern
vertically to create an angle of 120°
between the strokes of each X, the span
becomes considerably more open than
before. It is now open enough to allow
the pleats to be concertinaed flat.

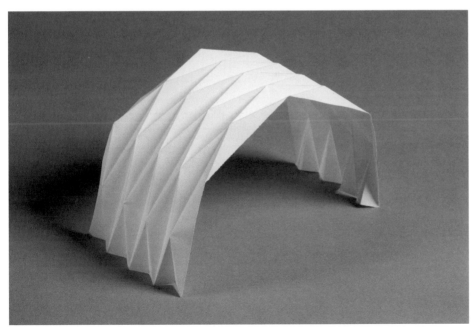

5.1 _ 4
Stretching the pleats vertically still more
to create an angle of approximately 130°
between the strokes of each X, opens
the span still more. As with the previous
example, the pleats will concertina flat.

5.2.   V-fold Spans

V-fold spans are created from V-pleats (see pages 102–135). Specifically, they use the Cylindrical V technique (see pages 130–132). V-fold spans are as versatile as the X-form spans on the previous page, and all the structures can be concertinaed flat. In contrast, though, V-fold spans create more box-like structures than X-form ones.

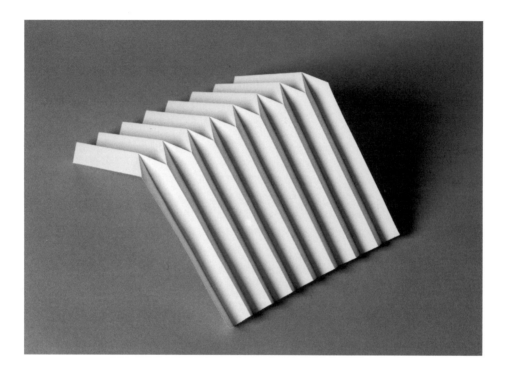

5.2 _ 1
A single line of V-folds is the simplest way to create a V-fold span, though the result is relatively crude. The angle between the strokes of each V shown here is 90°. However, the angle could be greater or smaller, thus opening or closing the span.

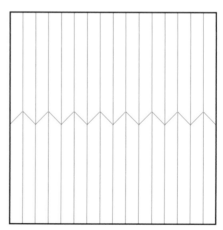

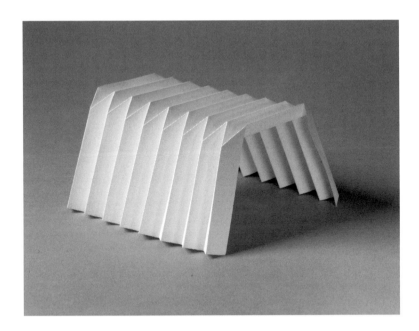

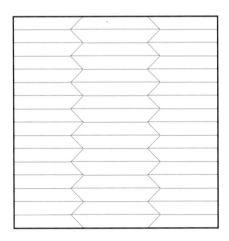

5.2 _ 2
The use of two lines of V-folds creates a
span with a flat 'roof'. Note how the two
lines are mirror images of each other.

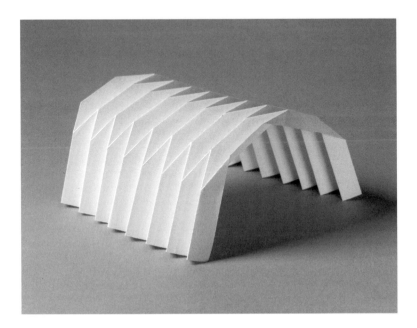

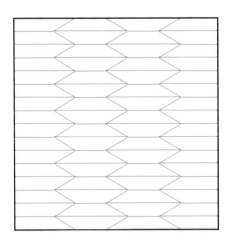

5.2 _ 3
Here, three lines of V-folds are used.
The angle between the strokes of each
V is 60°, not 90° as before, which
stretches the span and makes it
more open. This structure begins
to resemble the X-form spans.

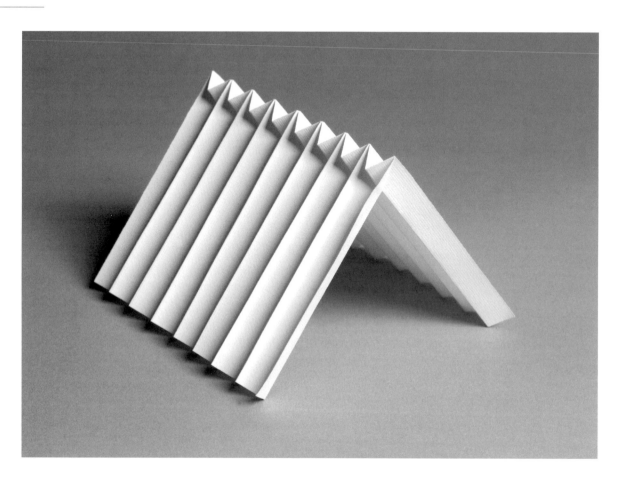

5.2 _ 4
This V-fold span variation creates
a square corner along the line of the
V-folds, instead of a filleted corner, as
before. Note the long horizontal mountain
fold, the valley Vs (not mountains, as
before) and how mountains and valleys
above the line of Vs remain the same
below the line.

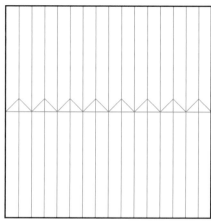

5.3.   Parabolas

Few would dispute the observation that of all folded forms parabolas (or more correctly, 'hyperbolic parabaloids') are among the most beautiful. They are also structurally complex to define, very strong and remarkably flexible. If you want to impress someone with a folded structure that fascinates both the eye and the mind, a parabola has to be a contender.

5.3.1 Basic Parabola

Here is the basic hyperbolic parabola. It is imperative to master this before you attempt any of the others. All the folds must be made with care so that every concentric square is made with great accuracy. If you become a little lost placing the folds and your sheet is messy, it is better to start afresh rather than continue.

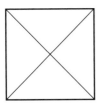

5.3.1 _ 1
On a perfect square, make both diagonals as universal folds (see page 8).

5.3.1 _ 2
This diagram is a copy of 1.1.1 _ 8 on page 18, which teaches you how to divide a length of paper into 32 equal divisions. Please turn to the page and learn (or relearn) how to do this. You cannot proceed until you know how to divide a sheet into 32.

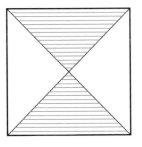

5.3.1 _ 3
Divide the sheet into 32, using the method described in the previous step. Notice three important things: how each fold is contained entirely within either the top or the bottom triangle; how no fold touches the edge of the square; and how there is no centre fold (the centre point of the sheet is defined by the crossing of the two diagonals).

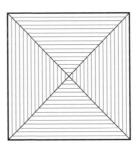

5.3.1 _ 4
Divide the other two triangles into 32. Make sure that each concentric square is made only of mountain or valley folds (not a mixture of the two) and that the squares alternate valley-mountain-valley-mountain between the edge of the sheet and the centre point.

How to Collapse the Creased Paper

5.3.1 _ 5
Starting at the perimeter, carefully fold the four sides of the largest creased square. To do this, hold the paper in the air, thumbs on the front and fingers on the back, and continuously rotate the paper like a windmill, folding the square bit by bit as you go round. Then, begin to fold the square inside the first. If the first square was a valley, this second square will be a mountain, or vice versa.

5.3.1 _ 6
Continue to fold square after concentric square, rotating the paper all the time. Note how each corner collapses to make a familiar V-pleat.

5.3.1 _ 7
After eight or so squares have been folded, the paper will begin to buckle – it will not want to lie flat. Note how a pair of opposite corners will gradually rise up, while the other pair will dip down. This is the start of the parabola. As you fold more and more concentric squares, the parabola will become more and more 3-D.

5.3.1 _ 8
Near the middle, the final few concentric squares can only be gently pressed and popped into place, not folded strongly. This is best done by making the paper more and more stick-like, rather than by trying to keep it flat.

5.3.1 _ 9
Eventually, all the concentric squares will have been folded and the paper will collapse into a narrow stick form. Press the four arms very strongly to strengthen the folds.

5.3.1 _ 10
Open the parabola by pulling the middle of a pair of opposite edges, then pulling the middle of the other pair of opposite edges. The more the parabola is opened, the more beautiful it will look. For transportation or storage, collapse it back to the stick form.

5.3.2.   Variations

Once the basic square parabola has been mastered, it is possible to make
many variations, using the same principle of dividing the sheet into 16 from the
edge to the middle. The greater the number of edges the polygon has, the more
flexible and fascinating the final parabola becomes.

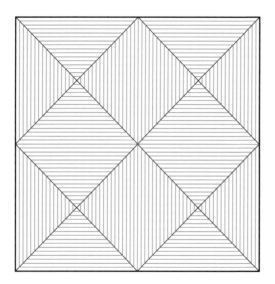

5.3.2 _ 1
A characteristic of the basic parabola –
and actually, any parabola – is that all
the edges of the sheet remain straight
and unfolded. This means that the edge
of one parabola can be fully connected
to the edge of another, allowing complex
structures to be built up from many
joined parabolas.

Not for the faint-hearted, this is a
one-sheet crease pattern for four basic
parabolas in a 2 x 2 grid, so that four
parabolas meet at the centre point.
The grid could extend infinitely. It is
possible to remove one of the parabolas
from the 2 x 2 grid and close the gap by
glueing the edges together, thus allowing
only three parabolas to meet at the centre
point. Similarly, five or six may be allowed
to meet at the centre point, or just two.

If you have the time and interest, it is
well worth making a dozen or more basic
parabolas and spending some time joining
them together temporarily in many
configurations. The possibilities are
immense and surprising.

5.3.2 _ 1
Instead of folding these
complex structures from one
sheet, the parabolas can first
be folded separately and then
joined temporarily with mini
pegs, paper clips or staples.
The example right shows four
separately folded parabolas
joined with pegs.

5.3.2 _ 2
For caption, see diagram
caption overleaf.

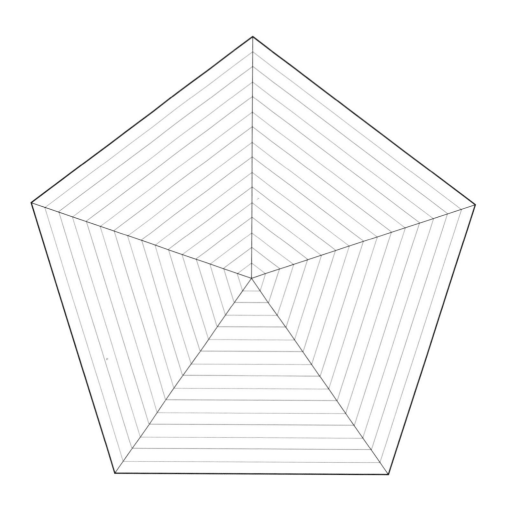

5.3.2 _ 2
Polygons other than squares may be
used, such as a pentagon. If you are
folding it by hand, you may need to draw
extra construction lines in light pencil
to help you keep all the folds parallel
and equidistant. Remember to play with
the final result – it is a very flexible and
strangely unresolved structure.
See photo on previous page.

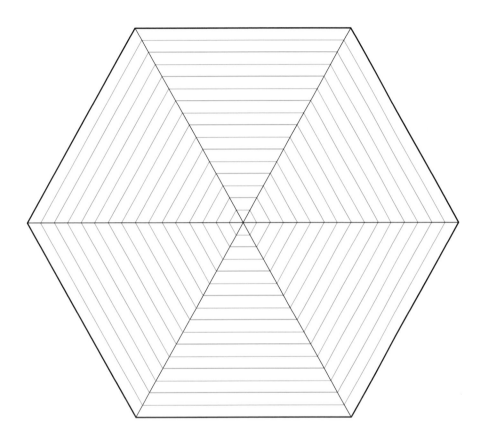

5.3.2 _ 3
The hexagonal parabola (above) is
particularly appealing. It is simple to
construct by hand and has the curious
property of flipping between a form with
three alternate corners on the floor (see
overleaf) and a form with four corners
on the floor, or two opposite edges.
Manoeuvring from one to the other
can be difficult!

The more sides the polygon has, the more
the corners can be flipped up and down
in different combinations to create an
increasing number of different forms;
the hexagonal parabola has just the two
described above, whereas the octagonal
parabola, for example, has four or five,
including forms which describe a cube,
tetrahedron or octahedron. As always
when folding, the key to finding these
variations is to play with the paper as
much as possible.

5.3.2 _ 3
A six-sided parabola
made from a hexagon.

6.   Boxes & Bowls

In origami, boxes and bowls abound. There are hundreds of different designs that could be described variously as boxes (lidded or unlidded), trays, bowls, bags, dishes, pots, vases or containers. Some are simple, square and functional; others are very decorative. They can be made from squares or rectangles, or from other polygons. Origami hats may be considered box forms, and vice versa.

The basic box-making technique is always the same: by folding, to reduce the flat 360° of material around a given point on the sheet so that it creates a 3-D corner, then to create more corners, connect them with folds and lock everything strongly in place. How the sheet is reduced from 360° to a smaller angle is the essence of box making. Making boxes is the art of making corners.

This chapter presents just a very few of the ways to make square, vertical-sided boxes. A little research will reveal many more.

Bowl forms are less like specific origami models in concept than boxes. Consequently, it is easier to create your own bowl designs than ones for boxes.

6.1. Boxes

6.1.1. Masu Box

The Masu box (see photo opposite) is a traditional Japanese design. It is a classic folded box; strong, adaptable, functional, and elegant in construction and final form.

The instructions here show how the classic Masu box is folded, and the following section, 'Masu Variations', shows how the same sequence of folds can create a family of different boxes.

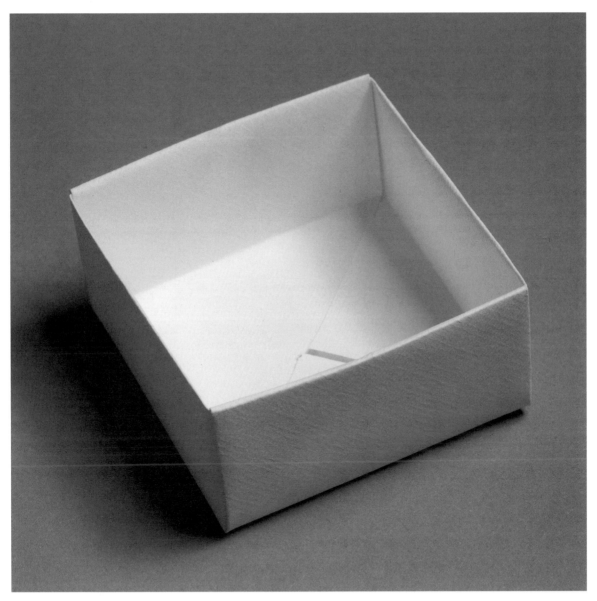

6.1.1 _ 15

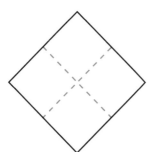

6.1.1 _ 1
Fold and unfold two
separate creases that
divide the sheet into four
small squares.

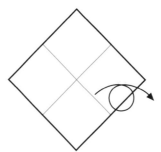

6.1.1 _ 2
Note the two long valley
folds. Turn the paper over.

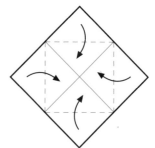

6.1.1 _ 3
The existing folds are now
mountain folds. Fold the
corners to the centre.

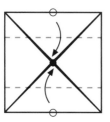

6.1.1 _ 4
Fold the top and bottom o
edges to the centre point.

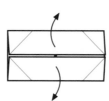

6.1.1 _ 5
Unfold Step 4.

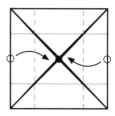

6.1.1 _ 6
Similarly, fold the left and
right o edges in to the
centre point.

6.1.1 _ 7
Unfold Step 6.

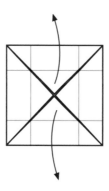

6.1.1 _ 8
Unfold the top and bottom
triangles only.

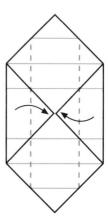

6.1.1 _ 9
Fold the left and right
edges to the centre line.

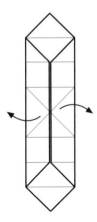

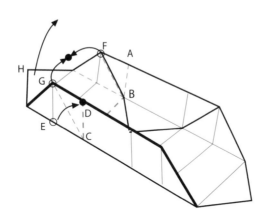

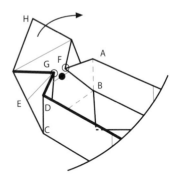

6.1.1 _ 10
Half unfold Step 9 so that
the edges stand up at 90°.

6.1.1 _ 11
This is the crucial step. Several things
happen at the same time. Corner H lifts
up to the vertical. Corners F and G come
together and touch. Crease A,B,C,D is
one long crease that defines the sides
and base of the box. E touches D.

6.1.1 _ 12
This is halfway. Note that H is lifting to
the vertical, F and G are almost touching,
the crease A,B C,D is now defined and E
is coming up to touch D.

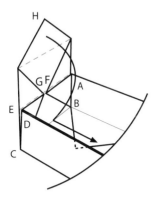

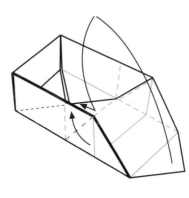

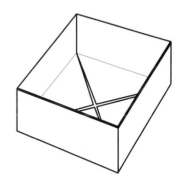

6.1.1 _ 13
The collapse is complete. H is vertical,
F and G are touching, crease A,B,C,D
has defined the end of the box and E
is touching D. Lock the end of the box
tightly by wrapping corner H over the
top of the box.

6.1.1 _ 14
Repeat Steps 11–13 with the other end
of the box.

6.1.1 _ 15
The Masu box is complete. Note how all
the corners of the original paper square
meet in the middle of the box.

6.1.2.   Masu Variations

The previous section gave the basic method for making the Masu box. However, by changing the position of the folds in Steps 4 and 6 (folding the edges to the centre point), the shape of the final box can be changed. Here are two examples.

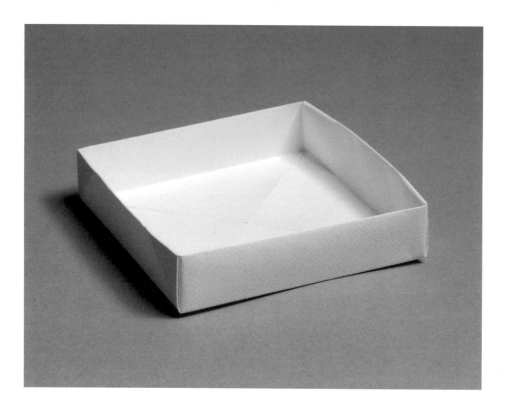

6.1.2 _ 1
Instead of folding each edge to the centre point, fold them to a pre-defined point closer to the edge than the centre. This will make a shallower box. The method for completing the box is exactly the same as for the basic Masu except that corners F and G will not fold in far enough to touch.

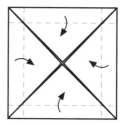

6.1.2 _ 2
Alternatively, fold each edge beyond the
centre point. If the folds are made along
the D divisions, the box will be a lidless
cube. The method for completing the box
is exactly the same as for the basic Masu
except that corners F and G will overlap,
not touch.

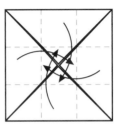

6.1.3.   Roll Box

The elegant rolling technique used here to create the box ends is a variation of the Box Spirals in 3.1.2 (see page 84). Many other box ends can be made by combining the examples shown in 3.1.2 with the example here. The box can be any length and only one end needs to be rolled closed – the other can be closed using another box-making technique, or simply left open.

6.1.3 _ 11

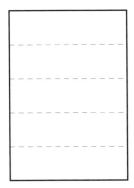

6.1.3 _ 1
Divide a rectangle into
fifths. An A4 sheet is a
good shape and size for a
first practice attempt.

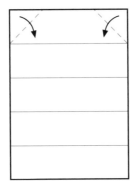

6.1.3 _ 2
Fold in the top corners to
the first crease.

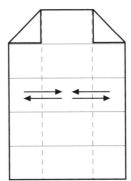

6.1.3 _ 3
Use the vertical edges of
the triangles as a guide,
and make two long vertical
folds. Open the folds.

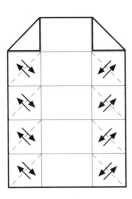

6.1.3 _ 4
Beneath each triangle
is a file of four squares.
Individually fold a diagonal
in each of the squares,
parallel to the folded edge
of the triangle above it.

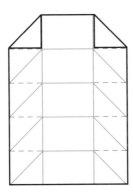

6.1.3 _ 5
Currently, all the folds are
valley folds. Refold the left
and right sections of the
four horizontal valley folds
as mountains.

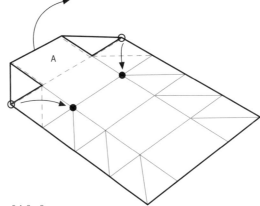

6.1.3 _ 6
The box can now be rolled
closed. Fold the top pair of
left and right diagonals, as
shown, rotating rectangle
A to the vertical. The sheet
becomes 3-D.

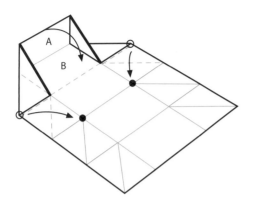

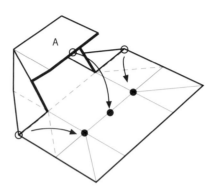

6.1.3 _ 7
Repeat, folding the next
pair of diagonals, so that B
rotates to the vertical and
A rotates to the horizontal.
Note how the two ends of
the box slowly create a
series of triangles, each
one on top of the one
made previously.

6.1.3 _ 8
Repeat again, further
rotating A and B.

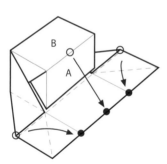

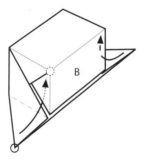

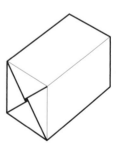

6.1.3 _ 9
Rotate A and B one final
time, to leave a pair of
triangles extending from
the box ends.

6.1.3 _ 10
Lock the box by tucking
the triangles under the
triangles connected to
rectangle B. This will
create a locked 'X' pattern
on the two ends of the box.

6.1.3 _ 11
This is the completed box.

6.1.4.　Corner Gather

The technique shown here for gathering and locking a corner can be adapted
to work with other polygons, not just a square. The sides can be made taller or
shorter relative to the base, depending on where the folds in Steps 1 and 2 are
placed. By changing the angles of the gather in Step 14, the sides can be made
to splay out like a bowl, rather than rise vertically.

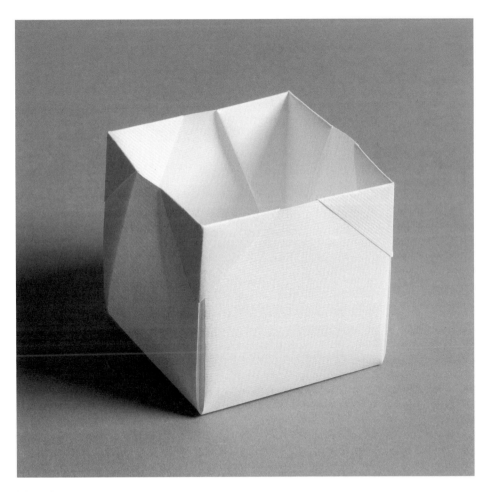

6.1.4 _ 16

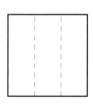

6.1.4 _ 1
Divide a square into
vertical thirds.

6.1.4 _ 2
Similarly, divide the
square into horizontal
thirds.

6.1.4 _ 3
Fold corner to corner
along a diagonal.

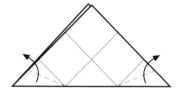

6.1.4 _ 4
Fold up the 45° corners, so
that the folded edge rests
along the one third crease
line ...

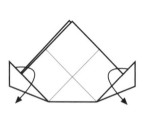

6.1.4 _ 5
... like this. Unfold the
small triangles.

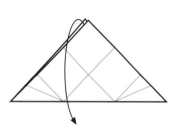

6.1.4 _ 6
Unfold the diagonal.

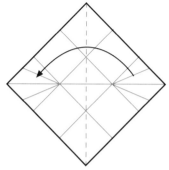

6.1.4 _ 7
Fold corner to corner
along the other diagonal.

6.1.4 _ 8
As in Step 4, fold up the
45° corners ...

6.1.4 _ 9
... and then unfold them.

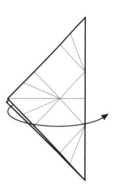

6.1.4 _ 10
Unfold the diagonal.

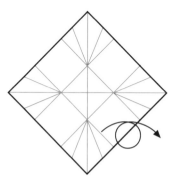

6.1.4 _ 11
This is the pattern of valley
folds made so far. Turn the
paper over.

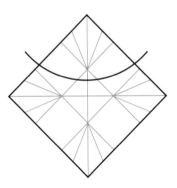

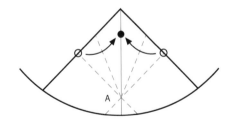

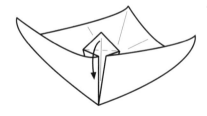

6.1.6.1.4 _ 12
The valley folds are all now mountains.
You are looking at the side of the sheet
that will become the outside of the final
box. The next step shows a close-up of
the top corner.

6.1.4 _ 13
This is the crucial step. Create separately
two valley folds from the small triangle
folds made in Step 4 or Step 8 (one is
already a valley, but strengthen it).
Then, fold the o circles to the ● circle,
allowing the two mountains and the two
new valleys to collapse simultaneously.
The paper will now become 3-D and make
a convex corner at A.

6.1.4 _ 14
This is now the shape of the paper.
Lock the 3-D gather by folding down
the top triangle ...

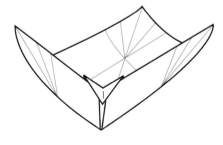

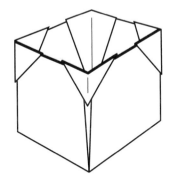

6.1.4 _ 15
... like this. The corner is now complete.
Strengthen the fold up the side of the
box and the folds along the bottom.
Repeat Steps 13 and 14 with the
remaining corners.

6.1.4 _ 16
This is the completed box. Further strengthen
and adjust all the folds until the box has flat
faces and straight edges.

6.2.   Bowl Forms

New bowl forms are easier to design than new boxes because the design parameters
are wider. For example, it is possible to change the ratio of the base area to the
height of the sides, change the square to another polygon, gather in the sides
a lot or a little to create bowls that are closed up or almost flat, and reverse many
folds from valley to mountain or vice versa, relative to other folds. When these
variations are combined in different ways, even the simplest ideas can create
many diverse forms.

The examples here represent ways to create bowl forms in a variety of styles
from the minimal to the ornate. Looking through the other chapters of the book
will provide you with many other ways to create shallowly indented corners,
which when repeated around the sides of a polygon will create bowl forms.

Of all the sections in the book, this one contains the ideas that can be most easily
adapted for a wide variety of sheet materials.

6.2 _ 1

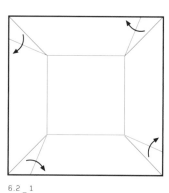

6.2 _ 1

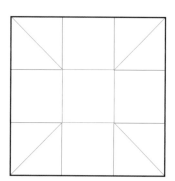

6.2 _ 2

6.2 _ 4

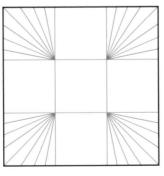

6.2 _ 3

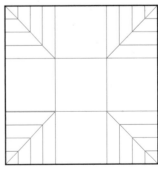

6.2 _ 4

6.2 _ 5

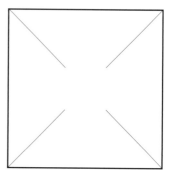

6.2 _ 6

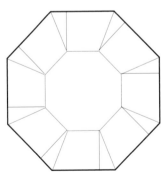

7.   No Crease, One Crease

It is easy to assume that a sheet with no creases or just one crease will offer very few possibilities for creative folding. It may even seem to be a preposterous idea.

While it is true that the possibilities for forms and surfaces increase with the number of folds, there is a surprising richness in using no creases or just one crease. The key to creating these forms is a non-origami technique called the 'Break', which induces curvature in the sheet. Ironically, with two or more folds and Breaks, the array of coexisting curves can quickly turn a sheet of material into an over-complicated doodle. If ever a folding technique needed to be used with precision and restraint, this is the one.

On another level, the extreme simplicity and directness of this technique offers a cleansing of the folding spirit when set against the examples in other chapters which require potentially dozens or hundreds of folds. In this way, No Crease, One Crease is not only a valuable technique, but also a respite from the rigours of complex folding. Less can be more.

7.1. No Crease

A 'crease' is a two-dimensional line. A No Crease is a one-dimensional point which creates a dent in the paper called a 'Break'. This generates complex curves in the paper, which can change from convex to concave and back again if the position of the curves is made to rotate around the Break. In this way, a simple Break – surely the most elemental of all manipulation techniques – creates not one form but many.

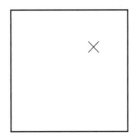

7.1 _ 1
Here is a drawing of the
Break, represented by an X.

7.1 _ 2
To make the Break, push
the back of the paper
at the chosen place and
simultaneously bring your
hands closer together to
create the convex curve.
When made with paper
about the weight of a page
in this book, the Break
takes form only when the
paper is held in the hands.
If it is released from the
hands, it will resume its
natural flat state.

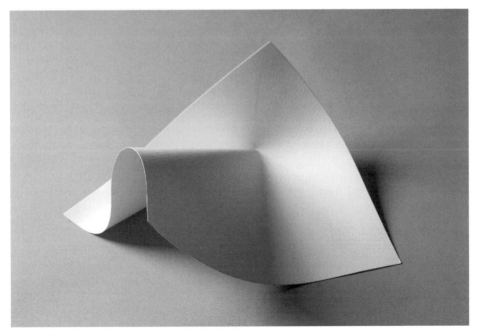

7.1 _ 3
When heavy watercolour
paper is used, wetted to
make it pliable and allowed
to dry (see 'Wet Folding'
page 186), the curves
retain their position.

7.1.1. No Crease Variations

With a Break placed almost randomly on a sheet, the paper can assume a number of different curved forms depending on which of the four edges is pulled forwards to create the predominant convex curve.

7.1.1 _ 2 _ 1

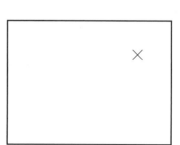

7.1.1 _ 1
The position of the Break on the sheet remains the same for the following six examples.

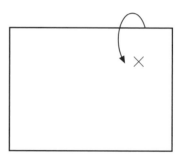

7.1.1 _ 2 _ 1
These drawings and photographs show how different forms can be made from the same Break when different parts of the edge are pulled forwards. The arrow on each drawing shows which part of the edge is pulled forwards and the corresponding photograph shows a possible result. With the Break in a different position on the sheet, other forms could be created. The paper is wet folded.

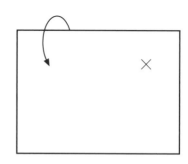

7.1.1 _ 2 _ 2

NO CREASE,
ONE CREASE
No Crease
No Crease
Variations

7.1.1 _ 2 _ 2

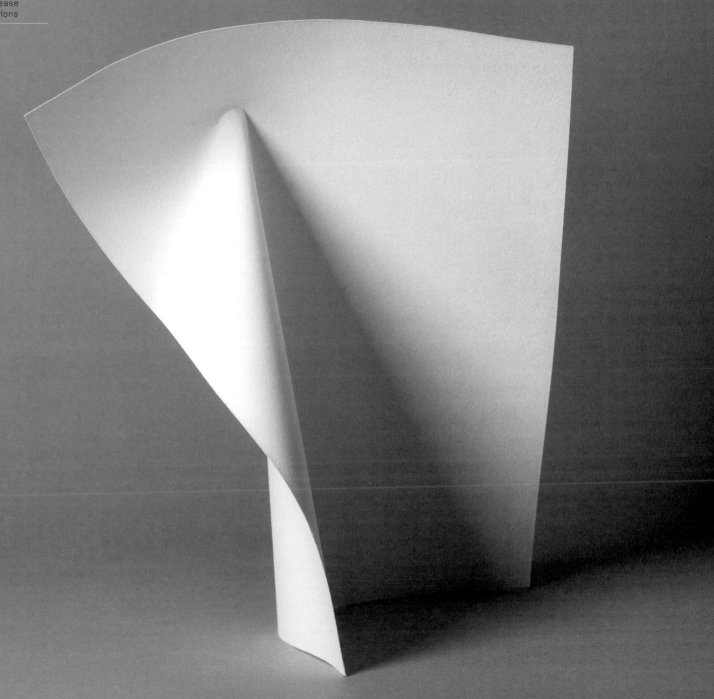

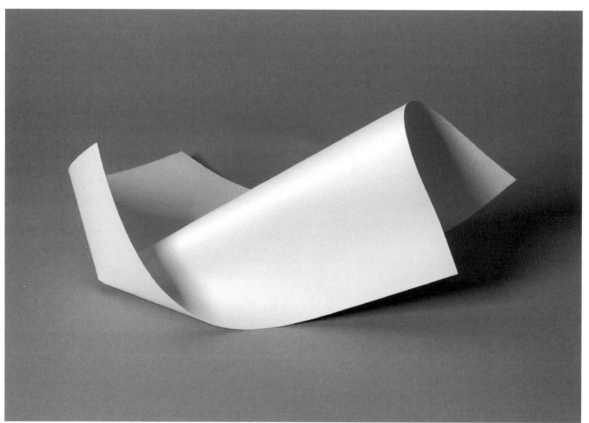

7.1.1 _ 2 _ 3

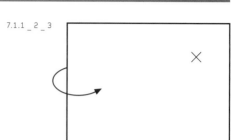

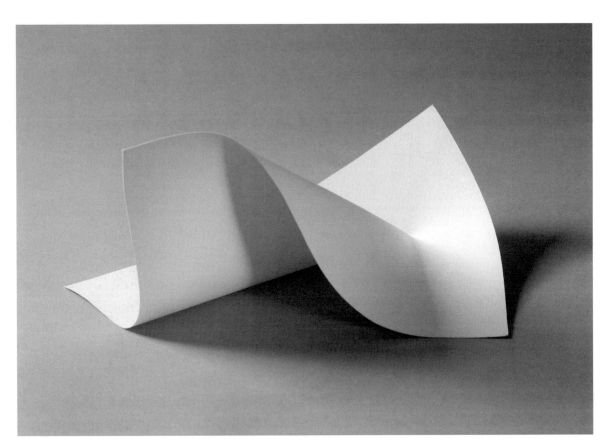

7.1.1 _ 2 _ 4

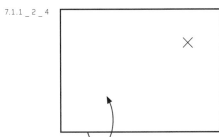

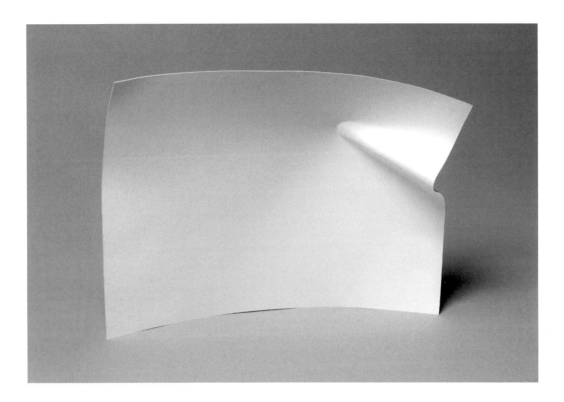

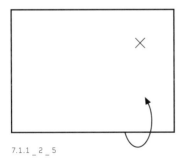

7.1.1 _ 2 _ 5

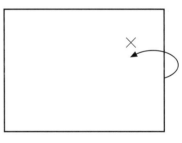

7.1.1 _ 2 _ 6

7.2. One Crease

With One Crease, the Break is made at a point along an existing mountain crease. In combination, the Break and the crease offer many more possibilities for forms than a No Crease Break. In the diagrams, the Break is represented by an X on a mountain fold.

7.2.1. How to Make the Break

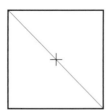

7.2 _ 1
This is the symbol
for a Break.

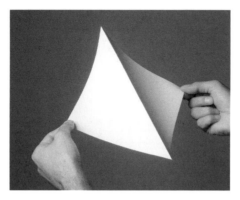

7.2.1 _ 1
Fold a square of paper along a diagonal. Open the fold and turn the paper over so that the crease is a mountain. Hold as shown, taking care not to flatten the crease.

7.2.1 _ 2
Pull your hands apart so that the middle point of the fold 'breaks'. Alternatively, rest the paper on a flat surface, mountain fold up, then poke the fold with a finger.

7.2.1 _ 3
Hold the two ends of the diagonal fold between your fingers and thumbs. Now bring together the two corners until they meet in the middle.

7.2.1 _ 4
Hold both corners between the thumb and finger of one hand. This will open two cones and allow them to be as rounded as possible. If the Break is not exactly in the middle of the mountain fold (or at another exact required place), it can be slid up and down the fold. Ideally, it should be a sharp point. However, if it has widened to become part of the length of the fold, holding the paper as in Step 3 and pulling on the two halves of the fold will sharpen it to a point.

7.2.2. Break Variations

The Break technique allows the paper to assume many positions. Here are
a few suggestions using the same diagonal crease and midpoint Break as
opposite. A useful creative exercise is to prepare about 20 squares of paper
with creases and Breaks in identical positions, then create different forms from
them. Use small pieces of sticky tape to fix them to a vertical surface. The range
of possibilities is immense.

7.2.2 _ 1

7.2.2 _ 2

7.2.2 _ 3

7.2.3.   Making the Break Permanent

Wet Folding

The technique of wet folding paper was developed in the mid-twentieth century by the great Japanese origami master Akira Yoshizawa, to create soft folds and rounded three-dimensional bodies for his representations of living creatures, without the folds springing open. It has since become the technique of choice for many origami artists.

Wet folding is best done with unsized or minimally sized papers such as watercolour paper, Ingres paper or etching paper. Suitable papers as heavy as 1000+gsm may be wetted and folded. When dry, wet-folded paper of any weight will become stiffer than if it had remained unwetted. The stiffening will be very slight on lightweight paper, but heavier weights will dry to become exceptionally stiff and durable. Wet folding is ideally suited to the No Crease, One Crease technique, enabling forms which spring open when made from conventional papers to retain their forms permanently. The pieces in this chapter have all been folded from 300gsm Canson watercolour paper.

Though particularly suited for the No Crease, One Crease techniques shown in this chapter, wet folding may be used to make almost any of the folded examples in the book, with the possible exception of the Crumpling technique in the final chapter. Made this way, otherwise flexible or unstable folded forms will become remarkably rigid, strong and durable. Even the highly complex V-Pleat forms can be wet folded, then bent into unnatural positions to dry, thus retaining a new and unconventional shape. The basic rule here is an obvious one; the thicker the paper, the stronger will be the final form. For extra strength, thicker weights of wet folded paper may be given a coat of polyurethane varnish.

Despite its advantages, wet folding has disadvantages too. The thickness of the paper and the stiffness of the final form mean that examples can look rather lifeless, even clumsy. In contrast, the lightness and springiness of thinner papers folded dry can give freshness and vigour to a folded form. Folding the same form both dry and wet will soon give you information about the pros and cons of both techniques.

However, if you have never tried wet folding, the technique is highly recommended, particularly if you are trying to create a folded form of some strength. In this way, wet folding can be considered a good mimic of other, stronger materials, such as clay or sheet metal and is useful for making mock-ups of concepts that may eventually be made in non-flexible materials.

7.2.3 _ 1
Fill a small bowl with clean water.
Then, using a viscose kitchen cloth,
apply water to both surfaces of the paper.
The thicker the paper, the more water
should be used. It is important to wet the
paper thoroughly without over-soaking it.
Make sure the work surface under the
paper is very clean and waterproof.

7.2.3 _ 2
As deftly as possible, make a No Crease (shown here)
or a Break. It is unwise to change your mind too often,
as bending the paper this way and that will compromise
the smoothness of the final curves. Speed and certainty
will ensure your piece looks its best.

7.2.3 _ 3
The wet paper must be kept immovable until it is completely
dry. It can be wedged tight between any combination of
everyday objects – bottles, cans of food, a wall, heavy books
etc. By allowing the paper to flatten a little here and tighten
a little there, it can be held in shape with a high degree of
precision. It is advisable to free the paper several times
during the drying to smooth out any buckles and perhaps
to adjust how it is being held.

Dry Tension Folding

If the paper does not hold its shape by being wet folded, it may – in some cases – hold its shape by being folded dry. Dry-folded forms with curved surfaces, such as No Crease, One Crease forms, are often highly unstable, springing open when released. However, additional small creases will lock the paper in place under tension. These are easy to make, although a degree of dexterity is needed to avoid 'crow's feet' (unwanted and unsightly buckles) on the pristine curve.

7.2.3 _ 4
Fold the paper to look like 7.2.1 _ 4 (see page 184). Turn it upside down so that the Break is at the top. Make sure the Break is a sharp point.

7.2.3 _ 5
With finger and thumb, squeeze flat the paper on either side of the Break. This will create a flattened triangle of paper. Try to keep the folds just a few millimetres long.

7.2.3 _ 6
Fold the triangle across to the left or right (the direction is not crucial), flattening it against one of the cones.

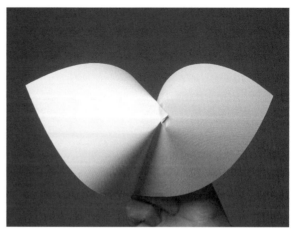

7.2.3 _ 7
This flattened triangle will now prevent the paper from springing open, though it will nevertheless relax a little.

7.2.4.   One Crease Variations

The Break can be made at any place on any mountain crease. Here are a few suggestions, though there are many others. It is important to remember that for every positional combination of Break and crease, the paper can be made to take many different forms, as shown in 7.2.2 (see page 185).

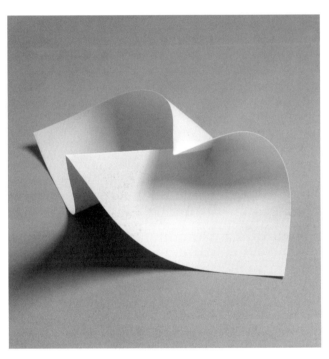

7.2.4 _ 1

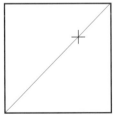

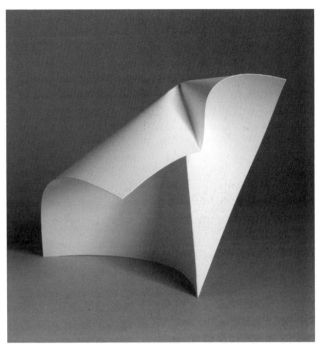

7.2.4 _ 2

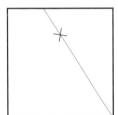

7.   NO CREASE,
        ONE CREASE

7.2.   **One Crease**

7.2.4. One Crease
        Variations

                                                                                7.2.4 _ 3

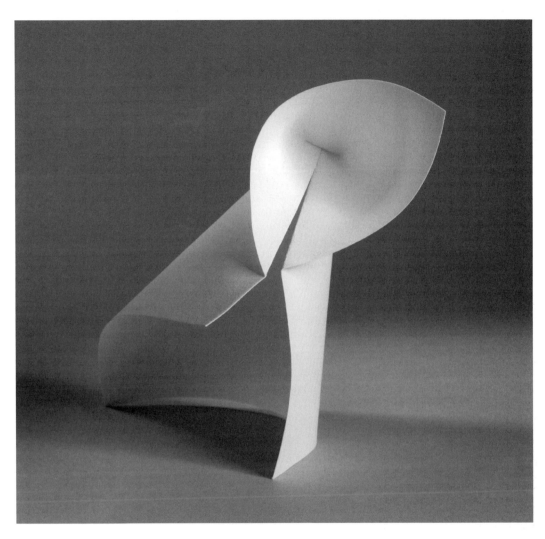

7.2.4 _ 3

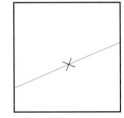

7.2.4 _ 4

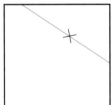

7.2.5. Less than One Crease

So far in this chapter, a crease has run from an edge or corner to another edge or corner. However, it is also possible to reduce the length of the crease so that it stops somewhere within the plane, or indeed, remains within the plane and does not reach an edge or corner. Here are a few examples, but, as always, there are very many more variations.

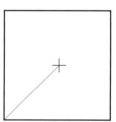

7.2.5 _ 1

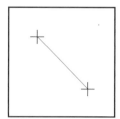

7.2.5 _ 2

7.2.5 _ 3

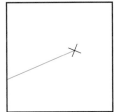

7.2.6.   More than One Crease

The natural tendency with the One Crease technique is to add a second and then a third crease to the sheet. Somewhat paradoxically, this will have only limited success! The curves induced by a single crease often conflict with those induced by a second, creating a sheet that is stressed and unresolved. So, when experimenting with the placement of more than one crease, consider where each one is placed with particular care.

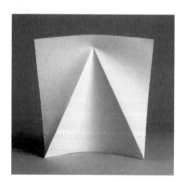

7.2.6 _ 1

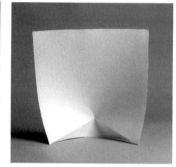
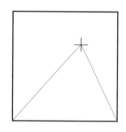

7.2.6 _ 2

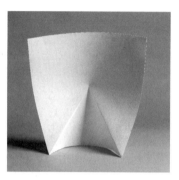
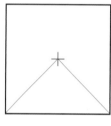

7.2.6 _ 3

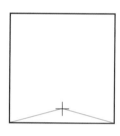

7.2.6 _ 4

NO CREASE,
ONE CREASE
One Crease
More than
One Crease

7.2.6 _ 5

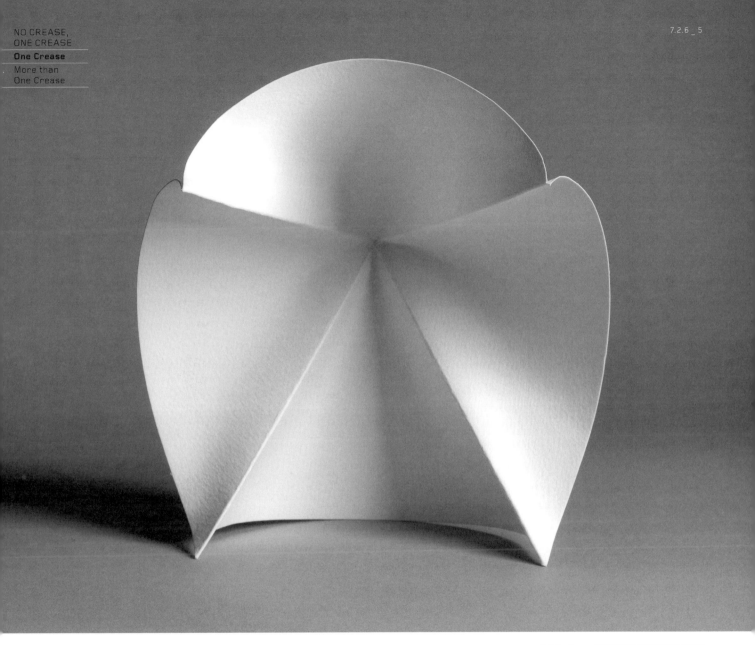

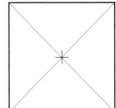

7.2.6 _ 6

NO CREASE,
ONE CREASE
One Crease
. More than
One Crease

7.2.6 _ 7

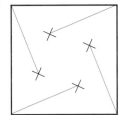

7.2.6 _ 7

8.   Crumpling

Crumpling is an exercise in controlled anarchy and an antidote to the geometry of the preceding chapters. It has a distinctive organic aesthetic that appeals to people who have a natural aversion to measured, geometric folding. It is also a technique much used by nature – think of flower petals that uncrumple as they open, our crumpled brains, crumpled rock strata and so on. What may at first seem to be a somewhat jokey folding technique could perhaps be the most profound. It is also the least explored and the least understood.

The essence of the technique is to carefully crumple a sheet to reduce its apparent size, then to expand it along certain lines or in certain areas by selectively opening the crumpled surface. It could be described as the simplest of all techniques – what could be simpler than crumpling paper? – but it is also the most difficult to do well. It requires just the right material and, as it is the most tactile and least mechanical of all folding techniques, a special sensitivity of touch.

If you are planning to crumple for an extended period of time, it is advisable to wear thin cotton medical gloves to prevent your hands getting sore.

Selecting Papers

Whereas most of the examples in this book can be made with almost any paper that will retain a fold, crumpling can be done successfully only with specific papers, or your results will be very poor.

The key factors in choosing a paper are weight and foldability. Papers below 60gsm are best. The thinner they are, the better they will be for crumpling. This is because thinner papers hold more folds, so the apparent shrinkage of the sheet when it is crumpled will be greater. However, not all thin papers crumple well. It is essential to use only ones that retain a fold, so papers

such as tissue paper, although easy to find, are usually of little
use. To find out whether a paper will retain a fold, crumple it
tightly into as small a ball as possible, using quite some force.
If it stays tight shut and opens only when pulled hard, it should
be good for crumpling. Another way to test for a good paper
is to hold a corner of the sheet and let it hang down vertically.
Shake the sheet vigorously. If it rattles loudly, it will probably
retain a fold well; if it is quiet, it will probably not.

Here is a partial list of suitable papers and sources:

Papers
- Onion-skin paper
- Bible paper
- Bank paper
- Gift-wrap paper
- Thin Kraft paper (brown wrapping paper)

Sources
- Paper merchants (for the papers listed above)
- Clothes shops (for the paper that wraps newly bought clothes)
- Wine merchants (for the paper that wraps bottles of wine)
- Florists (for the paper that wraps bunches of flowers)

If you are unable to find a good paper or have a spur-of-the-
moment urge to crumple, regular 80gsm copier paper will suffice,
though because the paper is a little too thick, the results will be
relatively unimpressive. Use A3 paper in preference to A4.
The examples that follow were made with 45gsm onion-skin paper.

8.1.   The Basic Technique

8.1.1. The Basic Method

This is the basic method for reducing paper to its crumpled state, ready to be stretched open.

8.1.1 _ 1
Crumple the paper into
as tight a ball as you can.
Use as much pressure as
possible! The photograph
shows the size of the
crumpled ball in relation
to the size of the
uncrumpled sheet.

8.1.1 _ 2
Carefully pick open the
ball until it is half open
and no more. Try to open
it evenly, all over. Note the
size of the half-open sheet
relative to the uncrumpled
sheet – it is about half the
area of the original.

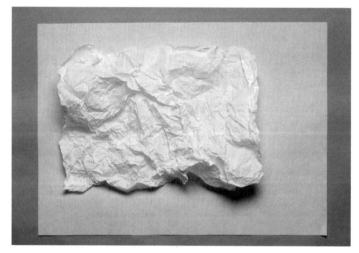

8.1.1 _ 3
Crumple the sheet again
into another tight ball,
using as much pressure as
possible. Again, half open
the sheet. The sheet will
be about half the area of
its previous crumpled size.

8.1.1 _ 4
Repeat the process once
again, crushing and half
opening the sheet. The
sheet will be about half
the area of its previous
crumpled size.

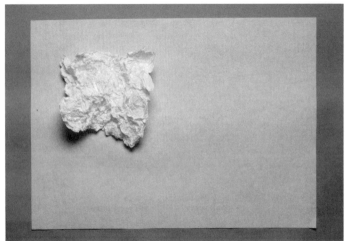

8.1.1 _ 5
Repeat the process once
again, and perhaps again
and again, depending on
several factors such as
the weight of the paper,
its size and how tightly you
crush the paper into a ball.

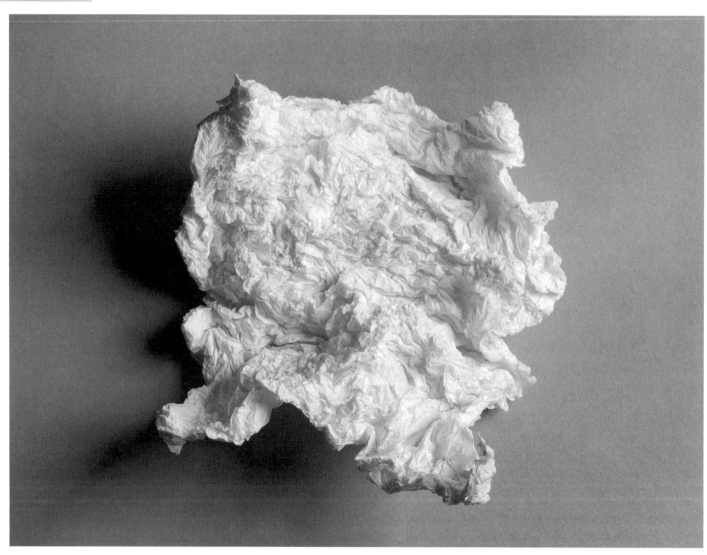

8.1.1 _ 6
The final crumpled sheet. The smaller it becomes, the
more dramatic will be the stretching, so it is important
to reduce the size of the crumpled sheet as much as
possible. However, the aim is to crumple it only until it
stops reducing in size. If the sheet is crumpled and half
opened too many times, it will become soft, the creases
will lose their elasticity and the stretching will not work.

8.1.2. Making Ribs

The crumpled surface can now be stretched open in two distinct ways. The first way
– to make ribs – is explained below.

8.1.2 _ 1
This is the basic rib. It is made by opening the crumpled
surface a centimetre at a time, then creasing the paper
as you go, creating a sharp, knife-like ridge. The effect
will be more dramatic if as little paper as possible is
opened (that is, uncrumpled) below the knife ridge, and if
the ridge is creased with some force, to make it as sharp
as possible. The ridge will not be straight and flat like
a conventional origami fold, but will create an arch.
The arch will curl more and more as the sheet increases
in size and as it becomes more tightly crumpled.

8.1.2 _ 2
When the technique is mastered, try making a number of ribs in parallel.

8.1.2 _ 3
Ribs can also be made
to meet at the centre
of the sheet, much like
an umbrella.

8.1.2 _ 4
Here, the ribs have
been formed to isolate
an uncrumpled square.
There are a great many
ways to organize a number
of ribs to create 2-D
surfaces and 3-D forms.
With just a minimal amount
of experimentation, a
surprising variety of
surfaces and forms can
be developed, from the
small to the monumental.

8.1.3.   Making a Mould

The other stretching technique that can be used with a crumpled sheet is to make a mould that follows the contours of an object placed underneath the sheet. With the right paper and good crumpling, a surprising level of detail can be achieved.

8.1.3 _ 1
Here, wooden cubes were placed under the crumpled sheet and the sheet stretched around them. Depending on the shape of the object underneath, a huge variety of abstract relief surfaces can be created.

8.1.3 _ 2
Moulds of recognizable objects can also
be made. Look around the room to see
what you can use! It is even possible to
make moulds of a face or a whole body.

8.2.   Linear Crumpling

The Basic crumpling method described on the previous pages reduces a sheet equally in every direction, so that it can then be stretched open equally in every direction. By contrast, the Linear method described here crumples the sheet in one direction, so that it can be stretched open primarily only in one direction. This means that the Mould technique described earlier cannot be used, though the Rib technique works particularly well.

8.2.1. The Basic Linear Method

8.2.1 _ 1
Roll the sheet into a cylinder with a diameter of
approximately 3–4cm. Hold it tightly in your left hand just
left of centre, then pull the right-hand half of the cylinder
through your tightly clenched right hand. Repeat, but with
your hands swapped. The result will be a narrow stick
with many parallel crumples. The photograph shows the
relative narrowness of the stick against the size of the
uncrumpled sheet.

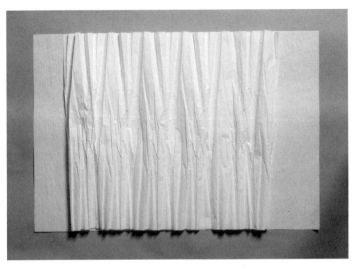

8.2.1 _ 2
Open the crumpled stick carefully. It will be about
three-quarters the width of the original sheet.

8.2.1 _ 3
Repeat Steps 1 and 2, being careful to press the folds
very tightly as the stick runs through first one hand and
then the other, and to only half open the stick. The stick
will open to be about half the width of the original sheet.
Repeat the process several more times, until the sheet
is full of parallel folds and will not absorb any more.

8.2.1 _ 4
This is the result. Be careful not to open and crumple the
stick too many times. Stop when you see the stick is full of
crumples and cannot absorb any more. This will maintain
the freshness and elasticity of all the creases.

8.2.2.   Linear Forms

As an alternative to the basic Ribs method described in 8.1.2, ribs can
also be added to a sheet filled with parallel crumples. They are best added
perpendicular to the direction of the crumples, because they become
increasingly invisible as they rotate towards the direction of the crumples.

8.2.2 _ 1
Ribs placed perpendicular to
the direction of the parallel
crumples create dramatic
forms. Mountain and valley
ribs may be placed together
in combination.

8.2.2 _ 2
Short ribs, or ribs of
various lengths, can be
placed on a 2-D surface.
Again, mountain and
valley ribs may be used
in combination.

8.3. Rotational Crumpling

After the Basic and Linear crumpling methods described on previous pages, Rotational crumpling completes the trio of basic crumpling techniques.

8.3.1. The Basic Rotational Method

8.3.1 _ 1
Hold the sheet at the centre point, allowing it to drape downwards. On smaller sheets, you might want to measure the exact centre, to ensure that the rotational effect is distributed equally within a relatively confined area.

8.3.1 _ 2
Hold the apex tightly. Pull the draped sheet firmly through the tightly clenched fist of your other hand. If the drape snags when it is pulled, straighten out the paper so that the crumples radiate neatly from the apex.

8.3.1 _ 3
Half open the paper, allowing the crumples to 'breathe' open.

8.3.1 _ 4
Repeat Steps 2 and 3 three or four times until the paper is full of as many crumples as it can hold.

CRUMPLING

**Rotational
Crumpling**

1. The Basic
    Rotational
    Method

8.3.1 _ 5
This is the finished
result. It is sometimes
possible to add more
crumples if the paper
is 'popped' inside out
between each repeat
of the crumpling.

8.3.2.   Rotational Forms

A Rotational crumple differs from the Basic and Linear crumples in that it makes
a 3-D form, not a 2-D surface. This means the vocabulary of possible forms and
surfaces differs greatly from that of the other two techniques.

8.3.2 _ 1
A spike can be created
by holding the apex and
splaying the paper out
beneath until a flat surface
is created.

8.3.2 _ 2
The rotational pattern of
the creases means that it is
difficult to create straight
ribs. Instead, circular or
spiral ribs should be made.

8.3.2 _ 3
If the apex of the spike is inverted into
itself and then opened, the spike form
becomes more button-like, as seen here.
If the paper below the button is gathered
up into a stick, the form becomes
remarkably like a mushroom.

8.4.   Advanced Concepts

8.4.1. 3-D Forms

Flat sheets were used for all the basic crumpling methods on the previous pages. However, crumpling can also be applied to sheets prepared as 3-D forms.

The easiest ones to prepare are simple geometric forms such as cylinders, cones or cubes. Use strong, liquid paper glue to hold the seams together and allow it to dry thoroughly before attempting to crumple the form. An overlap of 2cm is sufficient to create a strong seam. Prepare several simple, identical 3-D forms and crumple them using different techniques to see how they compare.

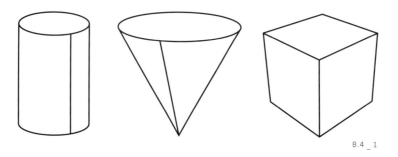

8.4 _ 1

8.4.2. Super-sizing

Crumpling need not be limited by the size of a single sheet. It is quite possible to glue many sheets together to create a surface or form of giant proportions. It is crucial to join the sheets together before they are crumpled, not afterwards. Curiously, the overlapped seams become almost invisible after the sheet has been crumpled, so super-sizing does not diminish the aesthetics of what is made.

Crumpling large sheets can be physically tiring and time-consuming, and is best undertaken by a small team of people. The results though, can be remarkable.

8.4 _ 2

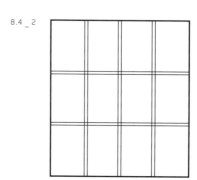

8.4.3.   Crumpling and Morphing

If you intend to create something of a specific size and proportion – for example, a crumpled medium-sized T-shirt – you cannot simply crumple a T-shirt from a medium-sized sheet. The result will be a much-reduced crumpled shirt, which would fit only a small infant!

The sheet needs to be much larger than the finished T-shirt, so that it becomes the required size when crumpled. Its size and proportion will depend on which crumpling technique is used (Basic, Linear or Rotational) and by what percentage it reduces in size when crumpled. To an extent, these calculations are best resolved by trial and error, though a ballpark estimation will provide an initial guideline.

The basic T-shirt shape will have to enlarge equally in every direction if the Basic crumpling method is used. However, if the Linear method is used, the T-shirt shape will have to enlarge and morph horizontally or vertically, depending on the direction of the parallel crumples.

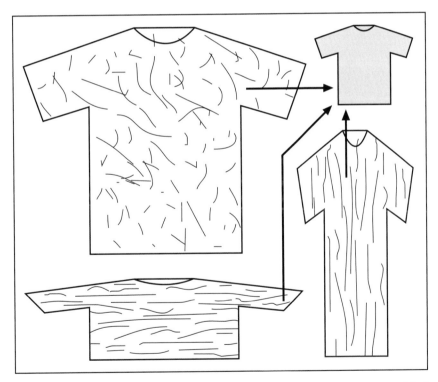

8.4 _ 3

8.4.4. Multi Layers

Instead of crumpling one layer, or perhaps a double layer if a 3-D form is
prepared (see page 218), it is possible to crumple through a multi-layered sheet.
First, fold the sheet into a simple 2-D geometric shape, then crumple it using
one of the methods described in this chapter. When opened, a complex pattern of
crumples will be seen, divided into areas bounded by straight origami-like folds.
Here is an example which creates a crumpled version of the Basic Parabola
(see pages 145–147).

8.4.4 _ 1
Fold a square of paper in
half along a diagonal.

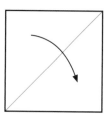

8.4.4 _ 2
Fold the triangle in half
again, to create a smaller
triangle.

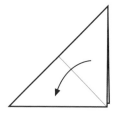

8.4.4 _ 3
Now crumple the four
layers as one, using the
Linear crumpling method
(see pages 210–211).
Note that the crumples are
parallel to the long edge of
the triangle.

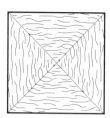

8.4.4 _ 4
Open the triangle back out
to the original square.

8.4.4 _ 5
When opened, three of
the four folds that radiate
from the centre point will
be valleys and one will be
a mountain.

8.4.4 _ 6
Carefully refold one of the radiating
valley folds as a mountain, so that one
full diagonal is a mountain and the other
is a valley.

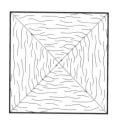

Now follow the technique used for the
Basic Parabola, which collapses a
geometrically creased square into an
X-shaped stick. Of course, the crumpled
square will not divide equally and evenly
into concentric mountain or valley
squares like the geometric version, but
you can nevertheless lightly gather up
the crumples as you go, working from
the perimeter to the centre point. Be
sure to create the buckled shape seen in
5.3.1 _ 7 (see page 146), making use of the
mountain and valley diagonals. Eventually,
the X-shaped stick will be made. Only
then should you crease the crumples
very firmly, strengthening all the folds.

8.4.4 _ 7
This is the result. Interestingly, it may take
a novice an hour to make the geometrically
creased parabola, whereas this crumpled
version should take only ten minutes.
In many ways, complex geometric folding –
especially folding which creates many free
points, such as some styles of complex
origami – can be considered a form of
controlled crumpling. 'Geometric folding
as controlled crumpling' is a concept rich
in creative possibilities.

FAQs

1. I have developed an idea which works well in folded paper, but doesn't work at all well in my preferred material of chiffon/hinged plywood/polypropylene. What should I do?

Adapting ideas that are successful in folded paper into other materials is always the most challenging part of the design process. The answer is to work more with the material you wish to use at an early stage, rather than coming to it only at the end of a lengthy process of working with paper. By doing so, you will come to know your chosen material better and find workable design solutions. You might even consider not working with paper at all.
Learn what your material is good at and work with, not against, those characteristics.

Some materials may not fold well, or at all, or may not hold a crease strongly, so you will have to find ways to keep them in place. Depending on the material used, this may mean adding stitches, starch, rivets, hinges, extra locking tabs, or laminating, welding, glueing, etc., etc. Additionally, much will depend on whether the design will be manufactured, by hand or mechanically, and whether it will articulate along the folded edges or remain immobile in a fixed position.

2. I don't want to use the ideas in the book because someone has already done them. How can I develop something original?

Late in Pablo Picasso's life, a journalist him how many original artworks he had created. He pondered the question for a long while and replied confidently, "Two!" The point, of course, is that in a long and brilliant career, Picasso considered he had had only two original ideas. Everything else was a reworking of those ideas, or of other ideas from borrowed sources.

It is the same for almost everyone else, almost all the time.
We take one idea from here, another from there, choose materials and technologies, add a pinch of creativity, stir everything together and so create designs which may not be 'original' but which take existing ideas and innovate them to make new forms – which in

turn may be used as references by future designers to create new forms...and so on through time. It's called 'research and development'.

Whereas simply copying something from this book may not be the best solution to a design problem, you can develop many new forms by combining elements from two or more examples, or by looking at the Basic Concepts chapter and putting an example in the book through some of the processes it describes.

So, the advice is not to throw away a book of potentially great design ideas in the search for something 'original', but to work with it, and combine diverse ideas, using the information in Basic Concepts. In any case, when you adapt an idea developed in folded paper into another material, it will change radically and will very probably be something no one has created before in quite that way.

3. I can't make the example on page XX. What should I do?

The usual tip is to put your work down, do something else, then come back to your work and look at it with fresh eyes. It often works! You could also try asking a friend for help. If you are trying to make something by hand, consider drawing it on a computer instead, printing it out and folding along the printed lines.

Alternatively, you could try to make the same example with fewer repeats, or even make it quite big (beginners often make things too small, which can be inhibiting).

Remember too that you don't necessarily have to copy an example exactly. If you have difficulty folding it, you may discover other forms that are more suited to your design needs. Don't be too locked in to the book.

4. I've found an origami model I want to use. Do I need permission?

This is a difficult issue. If the model is clearly assigned as 'traditional', it is in the public domain and you may use it freely. If there is no assignation, you should assume until you learn otherwise that it is a modern, authored work, protected by copyright. If it is assigned an author's name, it is protected by copyright. Artwork, even of a traditional model, is always copyrighted. If a design is protected by copyright, you must seek the permission of the author to use it. Many origami creators have an online presence and can be found easily. If you cannot find someone, perhaps because they come from a country which does not use your language or alphabet, it is often easy to find an origami association in your country or in the creator's country to help mediate for you. There are also online origami forums where experts can forward you to the right person or place.

However, you do not always need permission from the copyright holder. If, for example, you are a student doing a private college-based project, legally you do not need permission to use someone's work, though, as part of your project research, it is anyway a good idea to contact the copyright holder. If the work is later photographed for a magazine, placed on the internet, or otherwise publicly exhibited, you should seek permission beforehand. It is better to contact the creator at the start of a project to pre-empt the need to request permission at a later stage.

If you are a design professional working through ideas to show a client, it is best to work with the copyright holder from an early stage. If a copyrighted design is used, you may need to pay a fee or royalty to the copyright holder, or obtain a licence.

If you take an existing design and rework it so that it is sufficiently different, it can be considered an original design and you are the copyright holder. Just what may be considered 'different' is open to interpretation and you may want to seek the advice of an origami expert. All the designs in this book are generic techniques and are in the public domain.

A word of warning: in recent years several substantial out-of-court settlements have been awarded in favour of origami creators whose work was used without permission. A number of leading creators and authors have formed themselves into a group (Origami Authors and Creators) which monitors transgressions and takes action against transgressors.

In summary, it is advisable to find and work with copyright holders from an early stage. If you transgress the law claiming ignorance of copyright, or ignorance of the name of the copyright holder, or that you were unable to find the copyright holder, this is not considered a defence and you may be liable. As in all areas of life, early discussions will usually prevent later conflicts.

5.   Where can I find more information about origami and folding?

The easiest source of information about origami is the internet. There are hundreds of sites, large and small, informative and eccentric. Video posting sites and photo sites have a large origami content. There are also hundreds of books. Most major Western countries have well-established origami societies, and there are a growing number in South and East Asia, South America and elsewhere. They are easy to find online.

In truth, there is probably an over-abundance of sources and it is sometimes difficult to find quality, relevant information quickly amid the hubbub. Like all subjects worth exploring, finding what you need may take time, but it will be a fascinating, mind-expanding journey.

Finding information about folding as opposed to origami is more difficult. The online search engines are helpful, but the information is much more scattered than information about origami. You could also look through design and style magazines for examples of designs that use folding. Once you start to do this, you'll find many.

6.   May I send you images of my folded work?

Yes. I am always interested in receiving quality images of completed work in folded paper and other materials, though I probably won't have the time to enter into discussions about it.

7.   Are you available for workshops and consultations?

You can find my contact details online (enter 'Paul Jackson origami' into a search engine). However, I am not available to give advice and tutorials online.

The Author

Born near Leeds, England, Paul Jackson has been a professional paper artist and designer since the early 1980s. In a diverse career, he has written more than 30 books about origami and the paper arts, taught folding techniques in more than 50 colleges of art and design, undertaken many model-making commissions for print, television and other media, been a consultant for companies such as Nike and Siemens and exhibited his folded paper artworks in galleries and museums around the world. In 2000, he met and married Miri Golan, the founder and director of the Israeli Origami Center and relocated from London to Tel Aviv, from where he continues his international work.

Paul has a BA Hons in Fine Art from Lanchester Polytechnic (now Coventry University) and an MA in Fine Art from the Experimental Media Department at the Slade School of Fine Art, University College London. In the late 1990s, he took a sabbatical and gained a BA Hons in Packaging Design from Cranfield University.

Acknowledgements

I want to thank Barrie Tullett of The Caseroom Press for introducing me to Laurence King Publishing; the commissioning editor at LKP, Jo Lightfoot, for her enthusiasm for the project; and my editor Peter Jones for his diligence and great eye for detail. My thanks are also due to Meidad Suchowolski for his painstaking photography, and his assistant Behory Frish for patient hand modelling. I thank the book designers, &Smith, for their firm grasp of what the book was about and how this should be expressed visually.

I must also thank the late Bill Rickaby, my art teacher at Lancaster Royal Grammar School, for encouraging me to fold paper experimentally and to think visually – early lessons that defined my life as an artist, designer and teacher; the many heads of departments and lecturers in many polytechnics, universities and other colleges who have supported my teaching, particularly at Shenkar College of Engineering and Design in Tel Aviv, where I have run extended workshops and projects in many departments for some years; the many design professionals whose enthusiasm for folding has been inspirational; and last, but not least, my wife Miri Golan – who, in my wholly biased opinion, is the First Lady of Origami – for her support, patience and constant encouragement throughout the long preparation of the manuscript.

This book is dedicated to my students. You have always been my best teachers.

The CD-ROM

The attached CD-ROM can be read on both PC and Macintosh. All the material on it is copyright protected and is for private use only.

Numbers of diagrams on the CD-ROM correspond to those found within the book. The diagrams are arranged by chapter.

All diagrams were created by the author.